SPEED SECRETS 5

THE COMPLETE DRIVER

ROSS BENTLEY
AND BRUCE CLELAND

MOTORBOOKS

First published in 2005 by Motorbooks, an imprint of MBI Publishing Company, Galtier Plaza, Suite 200, 380 Jackson Street, St. Paul, MN 55101-3885 USA

ISBN-13: 978-0-7603-2289-5
ISBN-10: 0-7603-2289-9

Editor: Kris Palmer
Designer: LeAnn Kuhlmann

Printed in the United States of America

Contents

Acknowledgments

I've had the goal of writing a book on my list for far too long. With this in mind I first and foremost would like to thank my friend and colleague Ross for giving me the opportunity to share some of my thoughts and insights on the business of racing throughout the pages of this book. Ross and I have shared an extraordinary collaboration in our nearly 15 years of working together and I'm pleased to add this book as another milestone in what has always been one of the most satisfying working relationships in my career. Thanks Ross.

One of the themes you'll find woven into the concepts of this book is the idea of building a team of people who can help you meet your goals. I believe we've certainly done a good job of that in the Speed Secrets organization and our continued success speaks to the exceptional efforts of people like John Olsen, Gord Bentley, and the entire Speed Secrets coaching team.

In our efforts to bring the sales and marketing messages of Speed Secrets to the racing community, I would be remiss if I didn't single out the efforts of Ryan McCallen, our Driver Services Representative. Many of the sales and networking concepts in this book have been refined and executed by Ryan with "polite persistence." When it comes to selling, we really do practice what we preach. If you don't believe me just give Ryan a call and test him out. Ryan, we're lucky to have you on our team.

Lastly I would like to thank my first team, my wife Nancy and our children, Josh and Georgia. Throughout my career they've allowed me to pursue my passion for business and tolerated my indulgences in what some people call work.

—Bruce Cleland

Thank you to everyone who ever said "no" to me in my racing career. Thanks to all the potential sponsors, team owners, and anyone else who turned me down. I mean it—thanks for teaching so much. Oh yes, and thanks also to those who said "yes."

To thank every person I've learned something from about the business of racing would be impossible. However, despite taking the risk of missing someone very important to me, I would like to single out Tom Johnston, Dale Coyne, Craig Weatherbee, Joe Pruskowski, John Gorsline, Sylvia Proudfoot, Jeff Braun, Michael Gue, Tony Riddle, Kevin Benson, Gord Bentley, John Olsen, Ryan McCallen, and anyone else who influenced my knowledge and experience of the part of the sport that revolves around being outside of the cockpit.

The one person who has taught me most about marketing and the whole approach to the business of being a race driver is Bruce Cleland. As a sick form of thanking him, I invited him to join me writing this book—I hope he forgives me!

Over the past few years I've had the pleasure of helping direct, mentor, and influence the careers of a number of incredibly talented young race drivers. What I've learned in doing so is really the genesis of this book. Additionally, the parents of these drivers have taught me so much, and I'd like to acknowledge all of their input, deliberate or not.

Ultimately, you are the one that I most need to thank, though. If it wasn't for people like you who purchase the *Speed Secrets* books, I wouldn't get to figure things out by putting my thoughts and ideas on paper. Thank you!

The best thing that has ever resulted from my life in racing was meeting Robin, my wife, at the track. And the best thing that resulted from that is Michelle, our daughter. So, thank you to the sport of racing—not only for what I've learned, but more importantly, for bringing Robin and Michelle into my life.

—Ross Bentley

Introduction

Let us begin by stating the obvious: Getting paid to drive race cars is the greatest thing that can ever happen to someone with a passion for the sport. Most drivers who are making a living driving race cars would race for nothing. (To those drivers: Don't worry, we're not about to tell your employers!) So, to get paid to do something they love so much that they would do for it free, that's a good deal . . . no, a scam!

Our overall objective in this book is to help you get yourself into that position—the position where you are making a living driving race cars. Yes, your definition of making a living may be different from ours and, most likely, from Michael Schumacher's. But, whatever your definition is, it works for the purposes of this book.

We could give you a long, drawn-out recap of Ross' career and describe his background of not having any personal money to fund his career. He could tell you how, given that background, when he was first paid to drive a race car, he laughed inside his helmet while driving down the straightaway (it's true!). He could tell you how he has won some major races and championships, driven for some of the least- and best-funded teams in the sport, and made a living driving race cars for nearly 30 years. He could tell you how he achieved so many of his goals in racing through using much of the information we're going to present in this book. But he could also tell you that he's learned more from what didn't work in his career than from what did work. And we'll tell you what we've learned from other drivers—those who made it and those who didn't. All of this and more will be spread throughout this book.

A critical disclaimer, though, is that we don't claim to know it all. We have learned a lot about what doesn't work and a little about what does. While Ross will admit to certainly having some talent for driving race cars, he is the first to tell you that he may not be the most talented driver who has ever raced a car. And yet, he's done okay, making a good career as a race driver. The reasons for this are presented in the past *Speed Secrets* books, as well as in this one.

Throughout this book we will be referring to "making it." So let's define what we mean by that phrase. Or better yet, let's look at what making it could mean, because your definition is likely to be different from ours, or anyone else's reading this book.

To some drivers, making it means getting paid to drive a race car, whether for $50 or $5 million. They don't care what it is they race, as long as they can make a living doing it. For others, if they aren't racing Formula 1 (F1), they have failed. To them, it's not making a living that counts; it's being world champion that matters most. Others don't care much about what they race or whether they make any money doing it. What matters is that they are having fun doing it.

All of these motivations for working toward making it are different, and there are an infinite number of variations of these basic reasons. It doesn't really matter why you want to make it—at least not to anyone but yourself.

For the purposes of this book, though, let's agree on a basic definition of making it. We're going to assume that making it means making a living driving race cars, at a level (financial and a type of racing) that means something to you. Simple as that. In other words, it's how you define making it that matters. We're just going to throw that term out there, and you fill in the details.

It amazes us how many times we're asked by a driver to "help" him, to give him what he needs to make it to the next level of the sport. Usually, what the driver is really asking is if we can give him some money or where he can find some. Before you think that writing racing books makes us wealthy people—stop! Not only do we not have the financial backing to help you, we also really wouldn't be doing the best thing for you if we did. The best thing we can do is help you learn how to build a career.

Ross started his racing career by borrowing some money to buy a race car. It took a very creative and motivated speech to convince the bank that this rare "Ford built in England" with a three-digit serial number was real (without showing them a photo of it) and valuable. The loan officer couldn't quite understand why Ford had built a car with such a short serial number. Ross might have failed to mention that it was a Formula Ford race car—but then again, the bank didn't ask. He didn't think it needed to know that he could have written off its risk within a few laps. Again, the bank never asked if the car would ever see a racetrack, and he didn't think he needed to make the bank's busy working day more complicated by offering that information. The point is: if you want something bad enough, you will find a way. We're not suggesting doing something illegal or immoral. You don't have to do that, nor should you.

We also get a lot of young drivers who have won a lot of races and/or championships, or would have if such and such hadn't happened, and are upset because they aren't getting the breaks. They ask for help, because they think they are fast and they deserve to have someone pay for their racing. That's their attitude, as it is for many drivers. They think that since they have won some races, the offers should come pouring in. They should be driving F1, Indy, Le Mans, and NASCAR all at the same time with all the offers!

Many of those drivers see others getting some breaks and wonder, "Why not me?" The smart ones don't wonder for long. Unlike some drivers who approach us, the clever ones aren't bitter about the fact that they aren't getting these opportunities. Instead, they decide to do whatever it takes to put themselves in a position deserving of these opportunities and financial support. No, the dollars still won't flow in, but it will set these drivers onto a path that will lead to a good career.

Many drivers complain that they don't have a lot of personal financial backing, and that it's not fair that drivers born into the lucky sperm club (those with wealthy families) get all the rides. From personal experience, we know how frustrating this can be. However, it will be how you deal with this frustration and challenge that will determine your success in racing.

We've seen it many times and experienced it ourselves; drivers who have the ability and keep focused on what they want will make it somehow. Every one of those drivers have had to go through the frustration of seeing others who seem to have opportunities given to them, and the realization that it does take more than just being a fast driver and winning championships. It takes a lot more than that. Your ability to motivate people outside of your family to provide some support for your career is critical. Finding some way to fund your next steps is as important as your abilities behind the wheel.

You really have two options when looking at what we just wrote. You can get bitter and frustrated about it not being fair, or you can accept it and get on with making your career happen. You're not the only driver who is starting from where you are, and many others who have started from there have gone on to bigger and better things.

Simply asking for help will not work. There's a reason why drivers who came from backgrounds where they didn't have a lot of financial support make it. They used their passion, their commitment, their personality, their whatever-it-takes attitude to motivate and inspire people to *want* to help them. Simply asking for help is not enough; you need to find a way to motivate, inspire, and influence people to want to help. When you do that, you will find people who will give you those crucial opportunities. In fact, the first thing you should do is not to ask for help, but to ask what you can do for other people. Once you know what you can do for them, there's a better chance they will help you.

In the end—no matter what—don't give up. Get smart, use your passion for what you want to do, and find out what you can do for others to motivate them to help you. You can do it. If you are the type of person that other people like and respect, you will make it if you point your career in the right direction. This book is designed to help you find that direction.

Welcome to the business of being a race driver. The sooner you begin thinking and acting like a business, the sooner you will become a professional.

About This Book

One of the challenges of writing a book like this is that the state of the sport is constantly changing. When Ross wrote the first *Speed Secrets* book, he knew that the technique of driving a race car would not change too much. Sure, as cars evolve the techniques do need to change a little. That's one of the reasons for *Speed Secrets 2*. But choosing a series in which a driver, wishing to make a career in the sport, should race in is something that seems to change at least every year, if not more often. What was once the preferred path up the racing career ladder might not even exist a year later.

For this reason, we've tried to be series agnostic, just as we are when any of our Speed Secrets coaches work with a driver. In other words, we have no series preferences. All we care about here is that you accomplish what you want to in the sport.

We also cannot predict the future. (No big surprise!) We can't tell you what series you should race in a year from now for two reasons. First, that series may not even exist yet. Race series seem to come and go, and if it doesn't go away completely, it may have lost its attractiveness as a career-enhancing series. And that's the second reason we can't tell you what series to race in. A series that may be the best career move for you today may be a complete waste of time a year later.

The only thing that stays the same in racing is the fact that things will always change. So, we only refer to specific series when we have to make a point. Use our references to specific series only as a guide. We will refer to Formula 1, IRL/Champ Car, NASCAR, and Grand-Am/ALMS as the top levels of the sport. While no one can accurately predict what will happen with IRL, Champ Car, Grand-Am, and ALMS, they are the top levels of open-wheel and sports car racing in North America today. We will go out on a limb and predict the continued success of F1 and NASCAR for many years to come. (Brave prediction, no?)

Another huge challenge in writing a book covering this topic is that it is simply based on opinion. Writing books on driving technique, like the previous *Speed Secrets* books, is much more of an exact science. There is no way that a book explaining how to build a career as a race driver can be exact, and there will be some who will disagree with our opinions. Why? Because they have their own opinions based on their experience.

However, we've written this book to help you avoid the mistakes many others have made—including ourselves. In other words, we will help you learn from our mistakes and the mistakes of the many other drivers we've worked with, talked to, become friends with, and coached. We hope that this book gives you a clearer picture of what it takes to make it in racing and the steps you need to take along the way. We hope it speeds your climb up the racing career ladder. And we hope it helps you reach the level of racing in which you want to compete.

So, whether you're a driver wanting to make a career as a professional race driver, a driver that is already a professional, or an amateur who wants to be more successful or spend less of your own money, we hope to help each of you.

A crucial point: there is a big difference between your dreams and your goals. In our Speed Secrets business, we work with a lot of drivers who have strong and ambitious goals. In fact, we (our driver and career coaching) become a step, or an action, toward achieving those goals. However, we also have a few drivers who come to us simply with a dream. Typically this dream is to race in F1, NASCAR, Indy cars, or whatever. A dream is a goal with no action—no plan to get there—and that's what they have. Like our other services, this book is meant to help take your dreams and turn them into goals. It's meant to initiate an action, for without an action, all your goals are really just dreams.

SPEED SECRET #1

Use actions to turn your dreams into goals.

As in the other *Speed Secrets* books, we are going to risk insulting and alienating some readers by choosing to use only the male pronoun throughout the book. We apologize to all the female racers, but we're sure you will recognize that it's simply because of our male laziness (and to avoid the confusion of switching back and forth between she and he, her and him). Once again, this does not imply in any way that females cannot be successful professional race drivers. Far from it!

We're also going to make the assumption that you do not have more money than you know what to do with. In fact, we're going to base most of our advice in the book on a driver with little financial support. We figure that if you have more than an average amount of financial support, you will still need to know and use everything in this book, but you won't have the concern of finding the support to get to the next level.

The Job

To end this introductory chapter, let's define exactly what the professional race driver does. The job description is pretty simple. However, since there are two distinct places a driver performs his duties, the description is broken into two parts:

- On track: Drive the car at the limit—no more, no less
- Off track: Do everything you can to get back on the track as soon as possible and with the very best team and equipment

Our prior books, *Speed Secrets 1, 2,* and *3* were focused on the first part of this job description; this book focuses on the second. *Speed Secrets 4* was focused on those who help engineer the driver.

Chapter 1

Driver Types

More than one bench-racing session has been spent arguing over who is the best race car driver of all time. You may have participated in this discussion yourself. Names like Michael Schumacher, Ayrton Senna, Mario Andretti, Dale Earnhardt, Richard Petty, A. J. Foyt, Alain Prost, Niki Lauda, Jackie Stewart, Jim Clark, and Juan Manuel Fangio are most often bandied about in these sessions.

Over the past few years, our Speed Secrets driver coaches have also had this discussion, but mostly for a different reason. While it's a fun topic to debate, we are more interested in what we can learn from these greats. Fortunately, we have a pretty interesting perspective. Many of us have raced at a very high level and have even competed against some of these elite racers. We've also coached some young drivers who have gone on to distinguished things, such as winning the Indy 500.

Along the way, we developed the concept of The Complete Driver that was presented in the *Speed Secrets 2* book. But when defining what a young race driver needs to focus on to become one of the great champions of all time, we have also identified six different types of champion race drivers. They are:

1. The Workhorse
2. The Natural
3. The Charger
4. The Personality
5. The Professor
6. The Complete Driver

Let us define these driver types and provide you with some examples.

The Workhorse

The workhorse is a driver who has made it to the top and become a champion through a lot of hard work. He has developed his skills through practice and his career through hard work and determination.

When you think of drivers such as Bobby Rahal and Jimmy Vasser, Nigel Mansell and David Coulthard, or Terry Labonte and Ricky Rudd, you think of drivers who made it through hard work. Some say these drivers were not born with the same natural talent as others (although that is certainly an arguable point), but that they made it through their commitment, determination, and practice.

The Natural

Pure natural skill. Born with talent. That flair and skill that makes their speed seem to come so easily. That's what the natural has.

Ayrton Senna may be the poster boy for the natural, but others like Juan Pablo Montoya, Scott Dixon, and Casey Kahne have also shown the same innate talent.

The Charger

The charger tends to either win or crash. Attributed to big you-know-whats, bravery is often what he's credited with.

Gilles Villeneuve might have been the ultimate charger, but Paul Tracy certainly seems to have followed in his footsteps, as have Sam Hornish Jr. and Tony Stewart.

The Personality

Could it be that a driver has made it to the top due to his marketability and personality—simply who he is and how he deals with people around him? Or due to his lineage, like being a second generation driver? While a champion must always have driving talent, there are some drivers who have opened a few doors and generated some opportunities through their personality and the good fortune that has come with it.

Would Danny Sullivan, Jacques Villeneuve, and Michael Waltrip have had the opportunities to showcase their talents without their name and marketing abilities? Did Alex Zanardi and Damon Hill further their careers through their personalities or lineage? Without a doubt, they all have incredible driving talent, but there are certainly other attributes that have contributed to the personality's success.

The Professor

The professor types are thinking drivers. They often win at the slowest possible speed, using a calculated approach. Their cars are often better setup due to these drivers' analytical approach.

Jackie Stewart's strategy was to win at the slowest possible pace to conserve his car. Alain Prost, the F1 driver with the second most wins in the series, had the nickname "The Professor." Rick Mears might have been the very best Indy car oval racer ever due to his calculating approach to winning races. Even in the wild world of NASCAR, Alan Kulwicki won a championship by being just a little "smarter" than everyone else.

The Complete Driver

There have been very few drivers who are the perfect combination of all of the above traits, but that is the ultimate goal of every driver—or, at least it should be.

Michael Schumacher may be the most complete driver ever, although Mario Andretti might have been at least equal in his day.

- ☐ The Natural?
- ☐ The Workhorse?
- ☐ The *Charger*?
- ☐ The PERSONALITY?
- ☐ The Professor?
- ☐ The COMPLETE Driver?

What type of driver are you? Are you a natural, a workhorse, charger, personality, professor, or complete driver? Use the driver types to help you better understand your strengths and weaknesses.

Think about Schumacher: Is he a workhorse? Yes. He works harder at his craft than any other driver. Was he born with natural talent? Certainly. Is he a charger? Witness some of the dices he's had with Montoya, Mika Haikonnen, and Jacques Villeneuve over the years. Is he marketable and does he have a personality? Love him or hate him, Schumacher is a somebody, and his ability to motivate people around him is legendary. A professor? His attention to detail and his analytical approach is one of the keys to his success. The complete driver? Perhaps the best ever.

Although the definition of the complete driver has changed through the years, Mario Andretti is the only other driver in the history of the sport who we believe could rival Michael Schumacher in his completeness. He worked hard, had natural talent, was a charger, was marketable (who in the world doesn't know the name Andretti?), and was a smart driver.

Understand that we're not suggesting for one minute that one type of driver is any better than another. Nor are we saying that because a driver is dominant in one type, he isn't also strong in another. For example, the natural is no better than the workhorse, just because he may (or may not) have been born with more natural talent. You can argue that the workhorse, in fact, is better because he took what he was born with and made himself as good as the natural.

Neither is the charger any less intelligent than the professor, nor the professor any less assertive or competitive than the charger. It's just that each one has used his dominant trait to maximize his performance.

Now, if you had to pick one to be, it's obvious that being the complete driver is going to be advantageous; it increases your odds of making it as a professional race driver. Can you make it if you're not the complete driver? Well, the fact that so many champions have made it without being this type proves that it can be done. However, even the champions we've used as examples for each driver type are awfully close to being the complete driver. It's hard to find a characteristic that any one of them is weak in.

When you attempt to categorize a successful driver, you will notice that some are very difficult to identify as one type. That's because they are very well-rounded, or close to being the complete

DRIVER	DOMINANT TYPE	SECONDARY TYPE
Bobby Rahal	The Workhorse	The Professor
Jimmy Vasser	The Workhorse	The Professor
Sebastian Bourdais	The Natural	The Professor
Paul Tracy	The Charger	The Natural
Danny Sullivan	The Personality	The Workhorse
Rick Mears	The Professor	The Natural
Alex Zanardi	The Personality	The Natural
Gilles Villeneuve	The Charger	The Natural
Jacques Villeneuve	The Personality	The Charger
Ayrton Senna	The Natural	The Workhorse
Nigel Mansell	The Workhorse	The Charger
David Coulthard	The Workhorse	The Professor
Damon Hill	The Personality	The Workhorse
Scott Dixon	The Natural	The Professor
Sam Hornish	The Charger	The Natural
Helio Castroneves	The Natural	The Personality
Michael Waltrip	The Personality	The Workhorse
Tony Stewart	The Charger	The Natural
Jeff Gordon	The Natural	The Professor
Dale Ernhardt	The Charger	The Natural
Michael Schumacher	The Complete Driver	
Mario Andretti	The Complete Driver	

Just for fun, and to stir up some controversy, we have provided you with our opinion on a number of well-known drivers and suggested what primary and secondary driver types we think they are. Do you agree?

driver. The more complete a driver is, the greater his odds of success. Every one of the drivers we've listed here is close to being the complete driver. They are also all champions.

Take a look at drivers who have not won major championships and note how much easier it becomes to categorize them. The reason? They are not as complete. Coincidence? We don't think so.

Every young driver hoping to make a career driving race cars needs to look at his strengths and weaknesses. While the natural thought is to work on improving one's weaknesses and turning them into strengths, this is not always necessary or possible. Sure, one can make improvements and that's important. But, a driver also needs to focus on taking his strengths and making them even stronger.

There is a good piece of marketing advice that goes, "Differentiate or die." We'll come back to this later in the book, but for now let's relate it to your driver type. Being focused on what makes you different helps define your brand—who you are to the public, racing community, media, and sponsors—and a clearly identifiable brand makes it easier to sell yourself. It makes it easier for others to relate to and remember you. Focusing on your strength and emphasizing it may make it easier to build your brand, and therefore open doors to selling your services as a driver. For example, if you have a reputation for being a thinking driver (a professor), perhaps you can emphasize this and sell yourself to teams with this reputation.

How would you define yourself? Are you very strong in one area, but not so in others? Or are you a well-rounded, complete driver? Perhaps you're not sure. If so, ask people close to you and reflect on your racing experience. To which successful pro have you been compared to? Study that driver's career and see if any of the things he did to carry himself through the trial years into the successful ones would work for you. The more complete a driver you are, the more likely you are to become a great champion. What are you doing to become a more complete driver? Be honest. No matter how much natural talent you have, without being analytical and a charger, without having a marketable personality and working hard at developing all these traits, someone else with less natural ability and all the other traits will beat you. Think about that. Then ask yourself what you're doing about it.

Chapter 2

The Complete Driver

Speed Secrets 2 introduced the concept of the complete driver, so we won't go into great detail here. But we do want to review and emphasize it since in the last chapter we stressed how important this type is.

The complete driver is made up of the following skills:

- Racing
- Testing
- Physical
- Mental
- Marketing
- Career

Take any driver currently racing in F1, NASCAR, or Indy cars, but one who is typically running mid-pack or back. Let us ask: is the reason he's running in that position because he lacks the driving skills?

Look at our list of the six skills that make up the complete driver. Which of them is your example driver weak in? Which is he strong in?

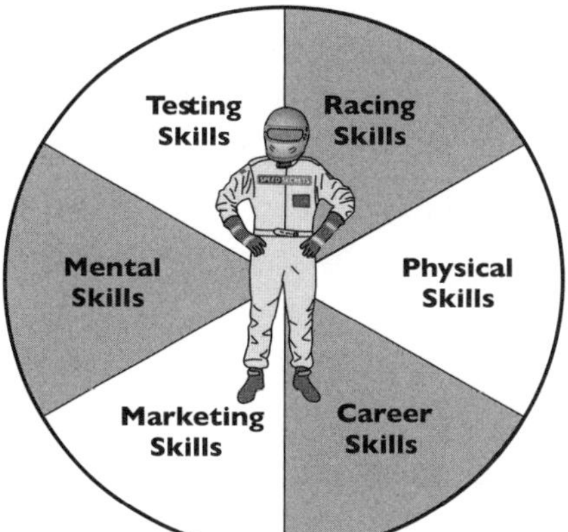

The complete driver is a balanced combination of six skill sets. The closer you are to having less weak ones, the better your chances of being a professional race driver are.

SKILL	TODAY	GOAL
Racing		
Testing		
Physical		
Mental		
Marketing		
Career		

As a test, rate yourself in each of these six categories on a scale of 1 to 10, with 1 being a weakness and 10 a strength. Then ask yourself where you need to be in order to meet your career goals and how you can do that. We recommend using this self-awareness test twice a year to chart your progress.

Now consider another driver and identify his weak and strong skills. Is he strong in racing skills, but not so in testing and marketing skills? Or is he strong in marketing and career skills, but not the fastest driver out there?

Now, consider Michael Schumacher. What are his weak and strong skills? Think about it. It's hard to find a weak skill, isn't it? He's a great racer, fast and brilliant when it comes to racing wheel to wheel. He's one of the best when it comes to testing and tuning his car. He may be the strongest ever when it comes to his physical and mental skills. Love him or hate him, he's a marketing person's dream come true. And he certainly has proven that he knows how to be in the right place at the right time—he has career skills.

The point of this exercise is to demonstrate that the more complete a package you are, the more likely it is that you will be successful. Michael Schumacher is so successful because he is so complete.

Note that when you rated the mid-pack drivers, you were still rating drivers that were at least in the pack. If you could rate some drivers who never made it, then it would be even easier to identify their weak points. In fact, the reason they didn't make it is just that; they had weak skill sets that let them down.

SPEED SECRET #2

The more complete a driver you are, the more likely you will have a successful career.

Chapter 3

What It Takes

There are five main factors to making it in racing, along with some minor ones. The five main factors are talent, commitment, money, people, and a plan. Have one without the other four and you will not make it. Have three without the other two and it's unlikely you'll make it. Even if you have four without the final one, the odds will still be against you. But having all five will provide you with a reasonable chance of becoming a professional race driver.

Talent

We use talent interchangeably with skill. It's what you bring to the driver's seat when you buckle in for a race. What we're talking about here is your ability to get around the track fast, not because of how fast your car is, but because of what's in your mind, your heart. You'll need your talent in every race, and it's something you can refine and hone through practice and study.

There are many people who will tell you that all you need to make it in racing these days is a lot of money and that anyone can buy their way into a ride. While we agree that you can buy your way in, it is your abilities behind the wheel that are going to keep you there. Even with all the money in the world, there is a limit to how far you can go with only a checkbook in hand.

What we're saying is, no matter what, you still have to be able to drive a race car—be fast, consistent, smart, and race well—to make a living as a professional race driver.

Did A. J. Allmendinger make it to where he is because of the money he brought? Absolutely not! While he and his family did take some chances and make some investment in his future, it was his ability as a race driver that got him to where he is now. How about Sam Hornish Jr.? Did he buy his way into his ride with Penske Racing? No way. He did have to pay for his rides in the junior formula, like Toyota Atlantic, but it was his ability to pedal a car that got him to where he is now. And Mark Weber in F1? Same thing.

One can make the argument that when given a choice between spending money on developing your driving abilities and helping you find more money, you should go for the driving abilities development. Sooner or later—preferably sooner—the people backing your career will want to see some wins. Refining your skills is the best way to get those wins. Drivers who win can bring in more money, drive faster cars, and keep the win cycle going.

How badly do you want to race? What are you willing to sacrifice to do it? These are questions you will have to ask yourself.

Commitment

When thinking about the question of what it takes to make it, we almost made a list of just one thing: commitment. Without the commitment to do whatever it takes to make it, all the talent and money in the world will not guarantee success. But if you are committed enough—meaning you have the burning desire and are willing to make the sacrifices necessary, and do whatever it takes—then you can develop the driving skills to go quite a long way.

No, we're not saying that with no talent and a lot of commitment you can make it to F1. But as long as you have some talent and work very hard at developing it, you can go a long way. How far will ultimately be dictated by just how much talent and skill you have and how you develop it. But without commitment, you'll never fully develop it, nor put yourself in the position to demonstrate it.

Far too many drivers with talent never fully exploit their abilities. They don't live up to expectations because they don't make the commitment. Often it is because they have some success early on and then think that they've got it, and therefore don't have to work at developing their skills. They think that the talent they were born with will take them to the top.

While having a strong belief in one's abilities is certainly a must, this kind of thinking and approach will usually fail. Nine times out of 10, a driver with a little bit of talent who then works hard at developing it will out-perform a driver with lots of natural talent that has not been developed.

Talent will only take you so far—it's what you do with your talent that matters most.

What you do outside of the car is just as important as what you do in the car. Ross once calculated the number of hours he worked at getting behind the wheel and compared them to the hours he spent behind the wheel. It was shocking. Even during one of his best years, when he spent the most time behind the wheel racing, he spent hundreds of hours outside the car for every hour he spent driving. If that's not what you had hoped for, then it's time for another endeavor. If you think that's unfair, find another sport. If you don't want to make that level of commitment, get out of racing now and save yourself a lot of time, money, and grief.

We have young drivers asking us all the time what they can do to make it in racing. Our first response is, "Do you have a girlfriend? Break it off. Do you have a street car? Sell it. Do you have a stereo? Get rid of it. Anything you own, sell it." That may sound harsh, but you need to be prepared to do these things. We're not saying that you will never make it while having a girlfriend or owning a car, but you need to be willing to do without them. You need to make the commitment, make the sacrifices. Ross once sold his street car to pay for an engine for his Formula Atlantic car after it had blown up the previous engine. Had he not done that, he would not have made the next race.

We also get a lot of people saying, "I've always wanted to race cars. . . ." To that, we think, "No you haven't." You see, if you've always wanted to race cars (or more to the point, become a professional race driver), then you would have done it. If it's something you've always wanted—that you would have given anything to do—then you would have found a way. Of course, if you're reading this book, there's a good chance that you've made a much bigger commitment to your goals and made more sacrifices than most.

To make these kinds of sacrifices, you obviously need to have the desire to make it—and badly. A lot of drivers talk about how badly they want it, but few make the sacrifices necessary to be successful. Few have the burning desire and passion it takes. Any wonder there are few drivers who truly make it?

We think passion is the key word here. Without the passion for racing—the absolute love of racing—it's doubtful you will have the burning desire to keep working at it. And without that, it's unlikely you will end up making a living driving race cars.

One last comment in this section, and it's aimed primarily at drivers coming from karting and moving up to car racing. Sell your karting equipment! The sooner you get rid of your karting equipment, the sooner you will be 100 percent committed to making it in cars. Some drivers hang onto their karts, thinking that they will use them to stay sharp while waiting for the big car racing deal to come along. And guess what? That deal rarely comes along. Why? Because as long as you have this fallback option of racing karts, you will not truly be committed to making the step up to cars. Of the young drivers we work with, only a few have the guts and smarts to make that level of commitment. And for those few, everyone can feel their commitment, and therefore will do what they can to help out. That's what commitment does.

Money

Okay, here we go. Here's the thing that most everyone will tell you that it takes to make it in racing. You've got to have money.

While it would be stupid if we didn't agree that it does take a lot of money to pave the way to the top, we are going to argue that it is not as important as many people would lead you to believe. We think the other factors here—talent, commitment, and people—are more important.

The list of drivers who have made it in racing without having come from a rich family, who paid their way, is impressive. In fact, if you were to look at the top few drivers in each major racing series in the world, you will find that the majority did not come from wealthy families. They found a way to finance their careers until they proved that they no longer had to provide any funding.

Having said that, money is important. You will need to find a way to have adequate financial backing to ensure you are in the right car at the right time. That may be your money or OPM—other people's money.

People

This may come as a surprise to you, but surrounding yourself with the right people is far more important than having the budget to pay for next season's racing. You see, if you have the right people around you, the budget will look after itself.

This is a lesson Ross claims to have learned too late in his career. He was so focused on finding sponsorship (he turned sponsor-hunting into his lifelong quest, it seemed) that he put no emphasis on the people around him. Then, one day it hit him (actually, an article in a magazine triggered his thinking); he needed to meet more people—people who could possibly help his career. Ross set a personal goal of spending the next year concentrating on networking with key people. No, he didn't stop looking for sponsorship, but it came second to networking.

A funny thing happened over the next year; he was able to secure more sponsorship. It seemed the more people he met, the more likely those people would introduce him to others who may know someone who knew someone. . . . And the next thing he knew, he had the opportunity to present his sponsorship proposal to someone who really had an interest.

One of the most amazing things to happen in Ross' career was when a group of influential people, whom he had gotten to know, all got together in a meeting room with one goal: to help his career. Within weeks he had his first CART Indy car ride arranged. And he didn't personally go chasing sponsorship. This was an important lesson for Ross, and one you need to learn from.

SPEED SECRET #3

If you surround yourself with the right people, your financial challenges will be taken care of.

Remember one thing though. You are the only person who can truly surround yourself with these people. Sure, a friend or family member can help, but ultimately you need these people to want to help you. You are the only one who can ensure that happens.

So, it's who you know, not what you know. If you want to secure financial backing for your next season of racing, focus on who you know.

Now, we're making one major assumption: you are a person who can and will motivate the people around you. But, if your personality is one that tends to stop people from helping you, then ignore everything we've just said about how important people are. Instead, buy your way into the next ride, and the ride after that, and the ride after that, and so on.

Ultimately, you must be a team-builder in every aspect of your career—with the crew working on your car, your sponsors, your family, and anyone who can help you. Ask yourself, "Who is on my team?" In reality, it is everyone and anyone who may have the slightest influence on your career, from a stranger you meet on a plane to the crew member fueling your car. Your job is to motivate every one of these people—your team—to assist you in achieving your career goals.

In other words, you need to do more than just invite people to join your team. You need to ensure they buy in to you—that they believe in you and are truly part of your team because they want to be. Without this buy in, they are no different than a spectator, just along for the ride.

SPEED SECRET #4

Surround yourself with the right people and your career will look after itself.

Most people in racing don't mind giving advice. For many, it's flattering that you have asked them for help. Sometimes that can lead to them becoming somewhat of a mentor to you. If you can have one or more mentors, all of whom want to see you succeed, your chances of success will improve.

A key is to not burn out your team. How do you avoid that? By asking for advice and then acknowledging it. On the other hand, the easiest way to burn your people out is by asking for advice, then never following it, and instead, taking the advice of someone else. Sure, your mentor will not always be right. But if you constantly ask for advice, but never take any of it, at some point your mentor is going to feel unappreciated, used, and ignored. Where's the reward for him?

SPEED SECRET #5

Continuously look at what you're offering your team. Ask yourself, "What's in it for them?"

Plan

All the talent, all the commitment, all the money, and all the great people supporting you will not guarantee success if you don't have a plan as to how to use them. This is a critical factor that many drivers miss.

We're sure you've heard the saying, "If you don't know where you're going, how are you going to know when you've gotten there?" The obvious starting point of any plan is deciding where it is you are really going. Is it getting paid to drive anything, is it F1, NASCAR, or being a driver/team owner? We don't care what it is, as long as *you* know what it is.

Once you have the end point, you can begin to plan how you're going to get there. How many businesses do you think would be successful without having a business plan? Not many. In fact, successful businesses spend almost as much time planning their success as they do executing their businesses.

How many race drivers do you think have a business plan, or some type of plan for reaching their career goals? Not many. That's a good thing for you, for if you take the time to develop your plan, you will have a clear advantage over the other drivers who do not.

You can hire a motorsport consultant to help you put together this plan, or you can do it yourself. The key things for you to determine are:

- What are your racing goals?
- Where do you see yourself over the next 1, 2, 5, and 10 years?
- How do you plan to reach your goals?
- What resources will you need to get there, which ones do you have now, and which ones do you need to develop?

If you take the time to think through these answers and write up a plan to achieve your goals, we guarantee you will be further ahead than most drivers. How badly do you want a career driving race cars? Badly enough to take the time to develop a proper plan? Are you a racing junkie—someone who will race anything, anytime, anywhere—or are you a racing professional, someone with a plan?

Of course, all the planning in the world is not going to guarantee success. Without executing this plan, you will not make it any further than if you never had a plan. You need to make a plan, then make it happen.

Other Factors

In addition to talent, commitment, money, people, and a plan, there are a few other factors that contribute to whether you make it or not. These include awareness, discipline, age, and ego.

Awareness is a crucial factor both in and out of the car. If you are not aware of what your strengths and weaknesses are, it's unlikely that you will consistently perform at a level where teams will want to hire you.

You must have the ability to be self-analytical about your driving abilities and your career. Notice we said self-analytical and not self-critical. Being critical of oneself is unproductive, whereas being self-analytical helps build awareness. Once you have awareness of how you are performing, your mind will do this almost magical thing: it will steer you toward a better performance. This is especially true if you have a strong mental image of what it is you are trying to achieve. For those of you who have read *Speed Secrets 2*, you may recognize what we call the Learning Formula—MI + A = G. If you have a mental image (MI) of something, and you add awareness (A) of how you are performing right now, then your mind will naturally guide you to your goal (G).

We've witnessed a definite correlation between drivers' level of self-discipline and their success rate. It seems most successful drivers are extremely self-disciplined. To some, this may come as a surprise, for they have the misconception that race drivers are wild, devil-may-care people. Not true. Most great race drivers are very deliberate in their approach to their sport, and that takes discipline.

This discipline leads to the level of commitment it takes to put in the thousands of hours of work for every hour in the car. Without that discipline, you will most likely be distracted into doing other things that do not lead to success.

It is interesting how many people not directly involved with racing believe that race drivers love being out of control. They think that's why they race—to drive out of control. Nothing could be further from the truth. Most great race drivers are control freaks. Of course, their idea of driving in control may be different from the general public's notion. From the outside, it looks as though they are, but in fact the driver is driving right on the knife edge between in control and out of control.

The same thing is true when they are out of the car. Most great race drivers have a need to be in control. They like a certain amount of structure, a certain amount of discipline. It's as though the control out of the car provides some balance against what they do in the car. It provides a sense of comfort.

The point is: you need to be self-disciplined in order to get the necessary things done. Racing is a business, and if you don't have the discipline for a successful business, you won't be successful. The other *Speed Secrets* books describe how the best race drivers seem to be almost fanatical about the care of their safety equipment. Their attention to detail is a sign of a self-disciplined race driver. You need to apply that to every aspect of your career, from your equipment care to the details of the business of racing.

Discipline is often the trait you need when making decisions about career moves. We can't tell you the number of drivers we've seen through the years who had spent the last bit of their budget for one more race and gotten nothing in return. If, instead, they had used that money to find more money, they might have been able to race for the rest of the season. Of course, they lacked the discipline to say no to driving another race; they were race junkies, needing to feed their addiction. While the desire and passion for racing must be respected, making smart decisions will take you further. Sometimes you need to say no to a race and invest that money into good business—into what you really need at that time. It may be more sponsorships, a coach to help your driving, an engineer to make sure your car is well-tuned for the next race, or one of many other options. The key is having the discipline to make smart decisions.

Is age a factor in whether you're going to make it in racing? Certainly. But some people put far too much emphasis on a driver's age. They seem to think that if a driver hasn't made it to Formula 1 or Indy Racing League (IRL) by the time he's 20, he's over the hill. Nonsense.

While there are advantages for a race team to have a driver who is very young (which we'll cover in a moment), there are some big downsides. Racing is a tough business. It requires a strong personality to stand up for what you believe in. Some drivers are just not ready at 18, 20, or even 25. Often, these drivers will have a parent or manager to do the standing up for them. The problem with that is they never really learn how to do it themselves.

When you look at this from the team's point of view, this is a positive; that's why we said there are advantages to a team having a young driver. The team can mold the driver. Some people would define this molding as taking advantage of or brainwashing the driver. In either case, the team gets what it wants because the driver's personality has not been set yet; it's not strong enough to assert what he wants. Therefore, the team can make the driver do and say what it wants.

We've seen drivers who were absolutely magic at a very young age, but then seemed to stall in their progression and never amounted to much. Others who were not so hot at an early age turned into superstars later on. The age versus driving ability or results is not that important to us, as we've seen just about every type of progression.

So, what's the best age to be at specific points along the career ladder? There is no right or wrong answer for that question. Yes, there are some drivers who have made it at a very young age, but others have gone just as far when they were older. We believe the whole discussion of age is relatively insignificant in comparison to the other factors that we have discussed.

The last point we're going to cover here is ego. To be really successful in racing, it seems a driver must have a bit of an ego. What we don't mean by ego is an attitude, and what we do mean is an inner confidence or belief in oneself. See, there is a fine line between being confident and being cocky. One is good and one isn't.

The key is being able to control your ego. If your ego gets in the way, you're bound to make bad decisions and perhaps de-motivate some of the people with whom you're trying to surround yourself. That's just to name a couple of potential problems with an uncontrolled ego.

Some people will say a strong ego is just self-confidence. In our experience, the people with big, strong egos are not self-confident. In fact, they are often trying to make up for a lack of self-confidence by bragging, talking a lot about and keeping the focus on themselves, and demonstrating just how big their ego is. That is much different from having self-confidence, or having a strong belief in oneself.

Balance

No matter who you are, you will have good days and bad days in this sport. There will be times when you will begin to wonder why things are so difficult and what you did to deserve the problems you're having at that moment.

There will also be times when things just seem to go your way. We've never been a believer in pure luck, but it does seem to be a factor sometimes. That is, until you look back and analyze what caused the good or bad things to happen. We can't think of a time when there was not some logical reason for what occurred. It often has to do with preparation, or the lack thereof. It sometimes has to do with the people involved. The point is: there is always some reason for what happens. Your job is to figure out why things happen the way they do, preferably beforehand so you can use it to your advantage.

It's important to keep in mind why you're doing what you're doing. The exact reason isn't really the point. It is important that you know why and keep that in focus. Especially when things are not going well, you must concentrate on why you're doing it.

Earlier we talked of the absolute burning desire and commitment it takes to be successful in racing. There is a downside to that. If you are too focused on the goal of being a professional driver, you may lose sight of the fact that you are a human being and, as such, you need to interact with other humans. If you are so shallow and narrow-focused that you cannot function outside of the sport, you may lose opportunities. In fact, you may not even see the opportunities. Keep an open mind, be objective about your career, and realize a balance is needed in everything you do in life. If you are too much in either direction—too committed or not committed enough—then you will not be successful. Balance is what we're talking about.

Chapter 4

What You Need to Know

There are many things that you need to know in order to make a living driving race cars. In this chapter we'll cover the basics.

Obviously, you must have the skills and talent to drive a race car. That's a given, for if you are not fast, no amount of marketing and career skills will land you a ride with a top team. Having said that, and assuming you can wheel a race car, you need all the other skills that make up the complete driver. And, you need a lot of knowledge. Let's look at how you can acquire, develop, and fine-tune those all-important skills and knowledge.

To develop your skills in and out of the car, you can rely on the following:

- Racing Schools
- Personal Coaching
- Mentors and Consultants

Let's take a look at these.

Racing Schools

Not all schools are created equal. There are racing schools that are designed more for the person wanting the experience of driving in a race, rather than really wanting to learn how to be a race driver. When choosing a racing school, do your homework.

Is the school geared toward the experience of driving a race car, or is it aimed at helping you achieve your goals? In other words, is it akin to a vacation experience—like an amusement park—or is it designed genuinely to impart a knowledge base on which to build a career?

Some schools are all about putting bums in seats, and the more the merrier. They're geared more toward quantity than quality. There is absolutely nothing wrong with that, since there's a need for it. In fact, it's these driving experiences that often encourage people to become bigger fans of our sport, and often even to provide financial support for some drivers. But, if you're focused on making a career as a professional driver, look for quality rather than quantity.

Consider the curriculum of the school. If a souvenir video, as opposed to a true learning video (in-car), is part of the package, it's unlikely that the program was developed for the career-minded racer. Things like souvenirs, while nice to have, are usually geared toward people who are taking the school just for the experience.

Don't be afraid to ask a lot of questions before signing up for a school. What types of cars are used, and how do they relate to driving a modern race car? What types of tires are on the cars? Gearbox? How are these things going to relate to what you plan on racing in the future? What's the school's safety record? What do graduates of the program say about the school? Has it really helped drivers become better, or was the school just a step for the driver to get a license? What is covered during the training program? Is it just driving, or does it cover other aspects of becoming a professional race driver? What has its coaches/instructors done—not just as race drivers themselves (which is, most of the time, unimportant), but in getting results for the drivers they've worked with?

Is the school's aim to get you into its system, encourage you to keep coming back for more sessions, and spend more money on it? That may or may not be a good thing for you, but it is important that you realize that some schools have this as a major objective. They may offer a very attractive initial price, but once in their system, the cost seems to grow and grow. If that fits your personal situation and the training suits your needs, then this is perfect. But know what you're buying into.

Other factors to consider are the number of instructors per driver; how often and what type of feedback is provided; whether the feedback is personalized or general; if in-car instruction is provided (for sedan-type schools); whether passing is allowed or taught; if they use data acquisition; and if skid pad training is available.

These are just a few of the many questions you could and should ask on top of the most obvious ones, like the cost, location, and timing. These three things also need to fit your personal situation. If the school is not interested in taking the time to answer all your questions, that gives you all the information you need.

Yes, providing the information and advice we just gave you may seem a bit self-serving. After all, Speed Secrets Driver Development Services provides training that answers all these questions very well. In fact, that is the basis of our program—providing training for the driver who is serious about his career. This may sound like an advertisement, but it's not meant to be. We're being as unbiased and honest as possible with all the advice we pass on in this book. We've always found that to be the most effective way of helping others.

Personal Coaching

Depending on where you are in your career and what type of racing you're involved in, driver coaching has either recently been accepted as something a driver needs, or people will look at you and ask, "Why do you need a coach?" It seems that in the junior formula car ranks—in the world of young drivers striving to be the very best and prove they belong in F1, NASCAR, or Indy cars—coaching is not only acceptable, but has also become a must. Sure, there are many young drivers who still don't feel they need a coach. They are typically the ones who had some early success and now either have the attitude of "don't mess with success" or "I've got so much natural talent that I'll never need someone to tell me how to do this." Both, unfortunately, are flawed thinking. Superstars are born with talent, and then they work to make that talent even better. Michael Schumacher is one of the hardest working drivers in the sport; he is constantly working to become an even better driver. (A little-known fact is that Schumacher has worked with the same coach for years. At least he did until the 2005 season.)

If you think to yourself, "I am the best," you probably don't need a coach. In fact, we doubt a coach can help you; you probably are not open-minded enough to learn more. (It's doubtful you will improve much from where you are now, as well.) But if you think, "I want to be the best," then a coach is a resource for you to consider.

So let's say you've decided you want a driving coach. You've probably come to this conclusion for one of the following reasons:

- I need to keep up with my competitors who have coaches.
- I want to get an edge on my competitors who don't have coaches yet.
- I think there is just a little bit more potential in me that I want to bring out. Yes, I'm good and I'm fast. And I know I can make my car better, but I think I can be even better. I want to be the best.

All three of these are great reasons for a coach. In fact, we predict that in the near future every serious race driver will have a driving coach, just as every serious race team has an engineer. It only makes sense since a coach can do so much to speed up your learning progression.

Okay, but how do you find a coach that is right for you? Again, we promise that we will provide this information in as neutral and unbiased a way as possible.

Let us first start by stating that the single, biggest challenge when it comes to coaching a race driver is that a coach cannot see the specific actions of the driver while he is driving. If he's observant, the coach can see the results, but not necessarily the cause. He can't peer into the cockpit and see exactly what you are doing as you drive around the track. Okay, there are times when a coach can ride in the right seat of a production-based race car to observe, but certainly not during a race; there are other (safety) limitations to this. A coach may be able to watch some in-car camera video, but that's rarely real-time. By the time he's observing the video, the race is typically over. So, a coach will spend much more time observing from outside the car than anything else. And that's where a good part of the problem lies, but not one that is impossible to overcome.

Coaching from the outside of the car is a bit like a basketball coach only being able to see whether the ball goes through the hoop, and then having to postulate on what caused the ball to go in or not. Did the shooter not follow through, or was his foot position wrong? Or, how about a golf pro only watching the ball land, and then having to figure out what the problem was with the player's swing? Having said all this, a great coach can easily overcome this limitation. It all comes down to his observation and coaching skills.

To select a coach, start by asking yourself this question: What do I want from a coach?

- Confidence-boosting?
- Morale-boosting?
- Driving technique instruction?
- Someone to talk me through corners over the radio?
- Someone who can help me focus better?
- Someone who can help me get into the mental state—that zone—where I drive great?
- Someone to help more with the mental aspects of driving, or the physical ones?
- Someone who can help me engineer the car?
- Someone who can read the data acquisition?
- Someone who can help translate what I'm feeling with and saying about the car, into something the team can understand in order to make the car perform better?
- Someone who can also help me develop outside the car—career advice, fitness, nutrition, and team selection?

Finding the right coach is critical; not every coach is right for you. You need to take as much time on deciding on a coach as you would when choosing which team or series you will run with. As you proceed to learn more about potential coaches and make a selection, there are numerous factors to consider. Other questions to ask are:

- How are his observation skills? Can he notice things from just watching me and the car go by that will help both of us understand what I need to work on?
- How well can he relate to me, where I am in my career, and what my goals and plans are for the future?
- Can we communicate well? How are his communication skills?
- Do I trust him, and does he trust and believe in me—both as a person and a driver?

- Does he deal with the mental aspects of being a race driver, as well as the physical skills?
- Is he more of an instructor, or more of a coach?
- Which do I need the most right now—physical skills or mental skills?
- How knowledgeable is he with data acquisition? Can he use it to help me?
- Is he able to work with the team on improving overall communications, team processes, and performance?
- Does he use a radio to communicate with me while driving, or does he wait until the session is over to have me think back to what I was doing?
- Is he a professional coach or an underemployed race driver wanting to stay near the track?
- Will his own personal racing experience help me, or is it not much of a factor?

The last question is a tough one. Just because a person has been a successful race driver does not mean he will be a good coach. In fact, very often it is the opposite. There are very good race drivers who do not have a clue as to why they are good, or are not good at communicating what you need to do. A great coach knows what is needed for you to perform better and can also communicate that to you, or at least help you figure it out.

There is another reason a driver with less ability or experience than you can be a great coach for you. A person with more expertise and experience will often just tell you what to do. You know what the problem is with that? Once he's not there to tell you what to do, there is a good chance you will need to be told what to do again! You will not have truly learned it. A great coach will help you learn things by guiding you to figure out the information or technique; by doing so, you will not need to rely on being told in the future. This ability doesn't require years of racing experience.

Of course, someone with a lot more experience than you may also have a tough time relating to where you are in your career. He may not be able to think like a beginner, and if that's what you are in relation to him, his perspective may not be very helpful.

So, while expertise and experience may be a benefit, it's not a must. Great coaching abilities are far more important.

Just as superstar drivers are born with some natural ability and then work to maximize it, coaches are rarely born great. The best ones have been trained in coaching. If the person you're considering as your coach only has his own driving expertise and experience as his qualifications, be wary. Even if he can back that qualification up with instructing experience, that's no guarantee. As with any profession, training and education—in addition to experience—are critical components. Ask your potential coach how much training in coaching techniques he's had. Of course ask a coach for referrals, talk to some drivers who the coach has worked with and see if their experience sounds similar to what you're looking for.

Mentors and Consultants

For a young driver on his way up through the ranks, finding someone else with experience in motorsports who can mentor you can be a key to success. Having someone who you can go to for advice on a career move, how you should approach a potential sponsor, or how to improve behind the wheel can be a great advantage.

Having been mentors to many drivers, we have a word or two of advice. First of all, the best way to de-motivate your mentor is to suck a lot of information out of him and then never even appear to consider it. We've spent many hours providing advice to drivers who promptly went and did the opposite of what we suggested. Then they came back for more information and proceeded to ignore our advice again. Now, we're the first to admit that we don't know it all, and that our advice may not be right for some. However, when we take the time to help a driver who then ignores everything we've suggested, it doesn't give us much motivation to go out of our way to help him again in the future. In such cases, we felt as though the driver was only looking for advice that fit what he had already decided to do. When that wasn't our advice, he ignored what we had to say and did his own thing.

When you seek advice from a more experienced professional, be sincere and have an open mind. Validation is not advice. Sure, a potential mentor may approve of the way you're approaching something, but that's not the only time you should listen to his response. Tiger Woods made golf's history books and set the sport on fire, but then he changed his swing while at the top of the game. Even though his performance suggested that he was doing things perfectly, he was open to ways of making himself even better. The point of seeking advice is to learn more. There are very few people, if any, who have no more to learn about their profession.

Again, we're not suggesting you have to follow every last detail of what your mentor suggests, but if you continuously dismiss what he has to offer, don't be surprised when he becomes reluctant to help again.

As mentors, our advice is that you look for someone whose career and skills you admire, go to them, and politely ask for some advice. For many people in the sport, this is an ego-boosting experience and they are happy to help out. But be respectful, both of what they can ethically tell you (there may be team information they cannot share) and of their time. If they are successful (and for your sake we hope they are), then time will be a big issue for them. If you take up too much of their time, your mentor may begin to regret having offered to help.

Also consider WIIFM—"What's in it for me?" While many mentors will never consciously ask this question, in the back of their minds they may be thinking about it. If you only ever take and never give, you may burn out your mentor.

Speaking of burning someone out. . . . Too many people within the sport follow the thought pattern of, "they are being born faster than I can burn them out." While that may work for some time, eventually your reputation will catch up and pass you, and it will be out there in front of you. It will precede you, and when you approach someone new for help or advice, your reputation will lead to a "no."

Other advisors and consultants to consider are sports psychologists, vision therapists, fitness trainers, nutritionists, hospitality people, public relations (PR) people, marketing people, managers, and media training experts. We believe that these are fairly self-explanatory in terms of what they do, but let's touch on the basics of what they can offer.

Sports psychologists can help you to get into the zone to be able to focus and concentrate better, as well as help you use visualization and get into a performance state of mind. Vision therapists, especially ones who specialize in sports, can be helpful, too. Most people will agree that you need to train your body to get in shape to drive, but very few realize you can do the same for your vision. After all, this is the most important sense you ever use while racing. Of course, fitness trainers and nutritionists can put together a program for you to follow on your own and help you monitor and fine-tune your training.

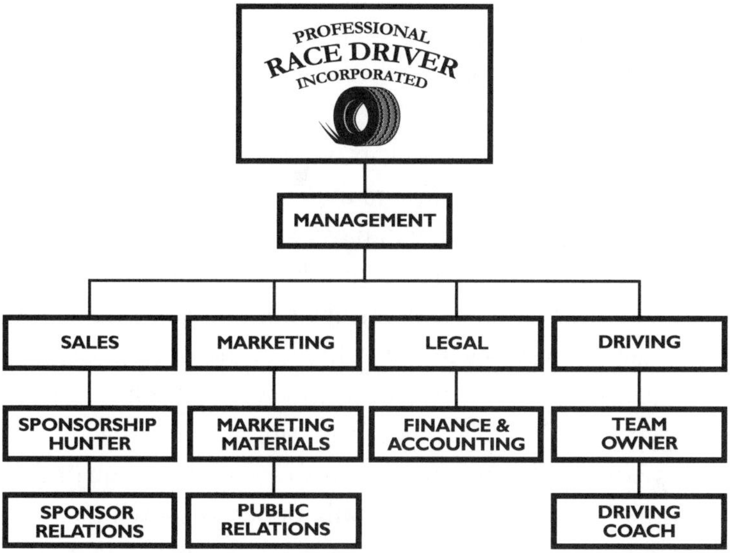

How is your team organized? Who is on your team? As a business, consider who you need to have on board to be successful and where they all fit in the organization.

The other resource people we mention here, hospitality specialists (to help support or entertain a sponsor), PR people (to generate exposure for you), marketing people (to develop sponsorship materials, prospect and sell sponsorship, or service the sponsors you currently have), managers (to assist in finding drives, negotiating contracts, and advising on career moves and decisions), and media training people (to train you in how to work with the media) will all be covered later in the book.

Consultants, who are new to this sport (at least in a formal sense, as many drivers, in the past, had mentors help in this area), are what you would call "career counselors." While a few coaches provide limited counseling, some go as far as developing career plans (mini business plans for the driver). Some also act as managers in that they coach the driver in all of the areas previously mentioned: psychology, fitness, nutrition, career, marketing, PR, and more. They are like one-stop career consultants.

The key to finding the right specialist is research; do your homework. Ask people who have been in the sport for a while, and some who are new (some old-timers are not very open to new approaches like managers, PR agents, and even coaches). And if you have a coach, you should be able to get advice and feedback on any or all of these advisors and consultants.

When considering any consultant, whether a coach, mentor, manager, PR person, or whatever, make sure they are more than just a fan. There have been many enthusiasts who have worked their way into the business through one of these roles simply to feed their love of racing. While the enthusiasm is important, it's not enough. In fact, they often cannot detach themselves from the hype of the sport in order to make good decisions and provide good advice. They can't be objective enough. What you need is a true professional—an expert, not a fan.

At this point we wouldn't want to suggest which one of these consultants is the most important. It really depends on which areas of the complete driver you need to work on most. It's important to know that all of these people are available and they can help you become more successful in your career.

Chapter 5

Career Steps

Career Directions

At one time in North American racing, the steps were relatively clear: you followed the road racing ladder from Sports Car Club of America (SCCA) club racing to the pro ranks, went from short track stock cars to NASCAR, or from sprint cars to Indy cars. It's not that simple anymore. There is much more overlap between forms of racing, with less of a standardized, accepted route to the top.

SCCA club racing is primarily a place for drivers wanting to race for fun, not to make a career. That's not to say one can't go from club racing to pro racing, but it's less likely now than in the past.

It used to be that oval racers were oval racers, stock car drivers were stock car drivers, and road racers were road racers, and there was very little crossover (with exceptions like A. J. Foyt and Mario Andretti). Then guys like Jeff Gordon and Tony Stewart went from sprint cars and midgets to NASCAR, and Sam Hornish Jr. went from a road racing background to being one of the best IRL oval racers.

Typically, for a young driver stepping out of the karting world now, the first step is into a race school series or a junior pro series. In both cases, they are open-wheel series, and these drivers will feel most at home with them due to their similarity to karts.

Like most things, when considering how to get somewhere, it's best to start with the end goal in mind. Ask yourself where you want to be, meaning what type of racing or what series you ultimately want to race in. It could be F1, IRL/Champ Car, Grand-Am/ALMS, NASCAR, touring cars, sprint cars, or something else. Or it could just be, "Anything, as long as I can make a living driving it."

If your goal is to race at the top levels of open-wheel racing, you need to spend most of your career driving open-wheel cars. If you intend to race closed-wheel production cars, you still should spend much of your early years in open-wheel cars. If you can be fast in an open-wheel car, you can be fast in anything. But the opposite is not necessarily true; just because you're fast in a closed-wheel car doesn't mean you will be quick in an open-wheel car.

If you want to end up in NASCAR, you should race stock cars as much as you can and start now. Get on the short ovals and learn how to race. Very few successful NASCAR drivers came from anywhere but the short track ovals.

If you take the approach that you're a road racer and you don't want to do any of that "boring oval track stuff," your career can be cut short. Of course, the opposite is also true. If you're an oval racer, the sooner you learn to road race, the better your career will be. Guaranteed. You will be a better oval racer if you learn to road race and a better road racer when you learn to race ovals.

Ross has raced both oval and road racing. His first season of racing was in a sprint car on short ovals. He then switched to road racing open-wheel cars and competed on ovals in both Formula Atlantic and Indy cars. Though they are different, one is definitely not more challenging or more boring than the other. Experience tells us that road racing is more physically demanding, and oval racing is more mentally demanding. You have more variables in road racing, whereas the precision and finesse in oval racing is greater.

The more oval racing Ross did, the better he got at road racing, and one of the reasons he has good race craft in road racing is because of his oval track experience. When he started racing long-distance sports car races, he became better in an Indy car. Every form of racing teaches you something that helps in the other forms. The more versatile you are as a driver and the more references you have to draw from, the better you will be.

SPEED SECRET #6

The more variety you have in your racing career, the more likely you are to make it.

The most important thing to keep in mind if you're young and just beginning your climb up the ladder is to drive. Drive as much and as many different types of cars as you can. Learn as much as you possibly can. Early on, you have so much to learn, and the best way to learn is to spend time behind the wheel.

So, what do you want to get from racing and your career? Do you want to race F1 or nothing? IRL/Champ Car or nothing? NASCAR or nothing? Anything with four wheels? Anything you can make a living from? You may also want to ask yourself, "What does making a living mean to me?" Is $25,000 a year a living, or do I want a million dollars a year? Does it matter? Is there a minimum annual pay you're willing to accept before considering yourself a real professional (one paid to drive race cars)? The answers to these questions will help you solidify your goals.

Getting Started

We don't know of too many drivers who start their careers without having to pay their dues, and we mean that financially as much as any other way. You will likely have to pay your way through the first few levels of the sport, as you probably already know.

So, that's the first stage to making a career—paying your way.

The second stage is the no-pay stage. That's where you no longer have to pay for a ride, but you also don't get paid.

The third and ultimate stage is the level where someone pays you to drive his car. Of course, you could be paid anywhere from just having your expenses covered to getting a percentage of the prize money, or from getting paid a small salary to getting millions of dollars a year. You could be paid by a team owner, a manufacturer, or a sponsor.

This third stage (where you get paid to drive) is when you can finally sit back and relax, right? Wrong! Once you're making a living driving race cars, your next goal is to continue doing that. That can be just as challenging as getting there in the first place.

We should clarify one thing right now: money is not the only reason to race. We keep talking about getting paid to drive, and how important that is. Most real racers are not motivated to race for the money. The only reason getting paid to drive is important is so you can focus just on racing. If you can get paid to drive and have any concerns about how you're going to pay your rent or your mortgage or buy your next meal, then all the energy you usually spend on those essential issues can now be put into your racing career. Getting paid to race allows you to do all the other things to prepare, like training. When you have to make a living in addition to driving, you can't focus 100 percent on racing.

Of course, there are people who race because they can make a good living at it. From what we've seen, they are the minority.

Once you reach that level where you are being paid to drive, you're in a different, dangerous world. Why dangerous? Because you can't go back—at least not if you want to stay in that world. If you've been paid to drive, and then you accept a drive for no pay, the word will get out that you'll drive for nothing, and you're back to square two, the no-pay stage. It's amazing how quickly a driver's reputation and credibility can change.

SPEED SECRET #7

The best way to get paid to drive is to be prepared not to drive for free.

You Pay Stage	Some Paid Stage	Get Paid Stage
At this stage in your career you're making an investment in the "product / brand" called you. You will likely need to self finance yourself through this stage because there are few business or marketing opportunites to attract sponsors.	At this stage in your career you should start to be a known commodity in the racing world. As a result, you should be able to demonstrate some value to both teams and sponsors alike and therefore should be able to generate some income from your program.	At this stage in your career you should be a well established brand. Organizations in and out of the racing world should see value in partnering with you. If you're still paying your own way at this point you should consider going back one stage and developing your skills / brand further.

You Pay Stage	Some Paid Stage	Get Paid Stage
No Audience	Some Audience	Lots of Audience
No Crowd	Some Crowds	Lots of Crowds
Few Business Opportunities	Some Business Opportunities	Lots of Business Opportunities

The path to getting paid to drive—to becoming a professional—has many factors along the way, such as the type of series you're competing in, the level of spectator interest, and the business opportunities available.

At some point in your career you need to be prepared to not race. That is, if you want to be a professional—and let's agree that a professional is someone who gets paid to do his job—you may need to say no. And you need to stick to that decision, no matter what. If you accept driving for free, then you are no longer a professional. More importantly, you also set a standard. You're telling the racing world that what you provide—your driving services—are worth nothing. If you're willing to accept nothing, then you must not be providing any value. That's the way it will be interpreted. It's as simple as that.

We realize there could sometimes be a long-term benefit to taking a nonpaying drive. But you need to believe that the long-term benefits are going to outweigh the short-term message you're sending—that your services are not worth anything. If you should take a nonpaying drive, at least send the team an invoice with your regular fees on it and a note saying something along the lines of "special discount." At least then you're establishing a value, and the team knows what you're worth and what they will need to pay next time.

Selecting a Series

After you first break into car racing, you'll have to choose, from then on, which series to compete in. Should you race one of the school series, rent-a-ride in a pro series, or set up your own team to compete in a series? And of those options, which series amongst them? Let's look at the advantages and disadvantages of each one, since we can't tell you what the perfect choice is for you.

Choosing a series can make or break your career, so you need to consider every minute detail. For instance, one consideration is how much of an impact you can make on the series and how much recognition you will get from it. This relates to what we discussed earlier in the book about driver types. If a particular series has many competitors of a specific driver type, and that's your type, perhaps you will make more of a splash in another series. For example, suppose you are a thinking driver and you're considering moving into a series that has a number of professor types. There, you might not stand out from the crowd as much as you would if you decided to enter a series where you would be the only professor.

We're not saying that just because there are a number of other drivers just like you in a series that you shouldn't race in it. But we are saying that it is another consideration. If you are close to saying no to a series, realizing that it would be difficult for you to stand out from the crowd in it should put the decision over the top, and thus make it clear to you that you need to look to another series.

SPEED SECRET #8

Look to a series where you can make the biggest impact—where you will get the most notice.

School Series

The advantages of competing in a school series are the ease, the equality of the cars, and the focus on your driving abilities.

Racing a school series is about as easy as it comes in racing. You sign up, pay your money, show up, get in a car, and go racing. If something goes wrong with the car, you get in another one. Even if you crash it, you pay for it, and get in another car. It doesn't come much simpler than that.

Without having to worry about the team, the car, or anything else, it makes it easy to focus on your driving and your development as a race driver. The school usually provides instructors to give you some feedback, so you can learn a lot if you're open-minded and you continually ask for feedback. The key here is that you may have to go looking for in-depth feedback from the instructors. It's one of the disadvantages of the school series: the quality and consistency of the instructors can be questionable at times. Some are very good; some are not. Some will give all the drivers a quick debrief after a practice session or race, and then leave. Others will spend good quality time debriefing you, especially if you show how keen you are to hear from them and learn.

The way we look at any of the school series is that they are as good as you make them. It's what you ask for that will determine your learning experience; it's up to you to make it a great experience.

While all the cars are supposed to be equal in the school series, no two race cars can or will ever be completely equal. Some series do a very good job of matching them. They test and tune them so that even if one has a stronger engine, the other cars balance out with handling or braking. Other series are not quite so concerned with equality in the cars.

If you feel you have a car that is not equal, then jumping up and down and complaining will not help. In fact, it may make things worse. The people running these series are human, and they can't help but lean toward people who are motivating. In fact, this is one of the most valuable aspects of running a school series—learning how to get what you want. In this case, it's how you make sure you are in the most equal car. If you sit back and just accept whatever you get, sometimes you will not get the best car. If you learn how to build a relationship quickly with the people running the series, you are more likely going to get what you want.

In the end, it is impossible to make all race cars completely equal. Outside of the schools, the cars' abilities will vary even more, depending on team budgets; crew chief and engineering abilities; aerodynamics; and other factors. In a sport where a few hundredths of a second make the difference, you are going to have to accept that a better car may beat you or help you beat others. But great drivers can make almost any car go fast, and that's what you need to focus on. Once you've got your ride, accept it and do everything you can at the wheel to get it around the course first. When you are struggling to keep up and you want to blame the car, our suggestion is to look at yourself first. Sure, the car may have a problem. But unless it's drastic, put the time and effort toward figuring out how to drive better instead of complaining. Nine times out of 10, a good driver can deal with what you're making a fuss about.

A lot of drivers will complain about the politics of the school series. Having spent a lot of time in and around many of these series, we'd be lying if we didn't agree that there are some politics, or favoritism. At the same time, we think it is less common than many would have you believe. Blaming the lack of results on politics is a lot easier—especially on the ego—than saying you're not as good as the driver who won.

The main disadvantages of a school series are the lack of a team and little or no ability to tune the car's setup. You can make the argument that focusing just on driving, and not worrying about tuning the car's setup, is a good thing. Generally, we would agree. However, an important part of the success of your career is in your testing skills, and that means learning the technical aspects of the sport. It means learning how to communicate to your team what the car is doing. It means knowing what a spring, anti-roll bar, shock, or aero change feels like. That knowledge is not something that you will develop in a school series.

Knowing how to work within a team is another critical aspect of your career. You will not learn this in a school series, at least, not like you would in a series in which you are one of two or three drivers on a team. Learning how to develop a relationship with your crew, how to motivate the members, how to get what you want out of them, and how to work with other drivers in your team are all things impossible to develop in a school series.

Rent-a-Ride

The main advantages to renting a ride with an established team in a series are:

- They know what they're doing.
- You don't have to worry about the operation of the team.
- You learn how to work within a team.
- You will be racing in a series where you are allowed to make setup changes to the car, thus learning about the car's technical aspects.

Usually, the teams participating in the series have been there for a while, and therefore have a lot of experience and knowledge. This knowledge is more than just how to set up and maintain the car. They also know the tracks the series runs, how to deal with the sanctioning body and series personnel, and how to handle the travel and team logistics.

Overall, the fact that you don't have to worry at all about the operations of the team and therefore can focus just on your own performance is a huge advantage. Running a team is a tough job, one that can distract from your driving if you have to deal with both.

One of the most important aspects of racing a young driver must learn is how to work within a team. While we will spend a fair amount of time talking more in depth about the details of what we mean by this, for now let's just say that knowing how to get the most out of the team is critical to your success. You play a huge role in making the other members perform at the highest of levels. If you can learn this crucial aspect early in your career, you will go a long way in the sport. While running your own team allows you to learn this skill, it can overload you as well; running in a school series does not give you the opportunity to develop this skill at all.

Compared to a school series, most junior formula series provide you with the opportunity to tune your car, even if it is still somewhat restricted for cost-control reasons. The sooner you learn how to read the car, how to communicate what you feel to your team, and begin to build a database of setup scenarios, the better. The complete driver is capable of sensing what the car is lacking in terms of handling, can tell the team exactly where it is lacking, and even has enough background to relate it to past problems. All this is only developed through experience.

The downside to renting a ride is simple: cost. That really is the only disadvantage, although making the right choice as to which team to rent a ride with is important. If you choose the wrong team, the whole rent-a-ride option will be a poor choice. We'll get into the how of selecting a team in Chapter 7.

Run Your Own Team/Car

As we've said before, running your own team is tough. It's a huge undertaking, one always bigger than anyone ever thinks going into it. We've never heard anyone say, "Wow, running a race team is a lot easier than I thought!" We've certainly heard the opposite, and if anyone ever tells you otherwise, he's either a fool or a liar.

You have to put a lot of focus and energy into running the team; therefore something has to suffer—your driving. If you're at the track and you have to answer to anyone about team issues, it's going to affect your driving performance. It's a fact of life.

We've heard drivers say, "Yes, but I have my father/friend/partner/whoever managing the team. I don't have to get involved." While that is a great intention, it rarely works out that way. The driver/owner will always have to get involved at some point, and that's true even if the driver is not the owner, but just the son/friend/partner/whatever of the owner. If it's *your* team, you will have to put some focus into it, and that will detract somewhat from your driving.

The advantages of running your own team in a junior formula series, in addition to the ability to develop car setup skills, are what you learn about the operation of a race team, the fact that you have control over the team, and that you can control costs. Of course, we don't know if anyone will ever truly be able to control costs in racing. We've also seen more people start off with the plan to spend less money than if they had rented a ride with an established team, and end up spending even more. In fact, this is more common than you probably think.

We've seen racers have mechanical failures that ultimately have resulted in a more expensive season than a rent-a-ride. We've seen driver/owners crash more, because they were trying to make up for a lack of a competitive setup. We've seen self-run teams spend more because they didn't have the experience or the inside knowledge on how to save costs. All in all, these teams ended up spending a lot more money "nickel and dime-ing" themselves than they were originally quoted by a rental team.

Of course, if you have the financial self-discipline, you can control your costs and even choose not to run the last race of a season if

	PLUSES	**MINUSES**
School Series		
Rent - A - Ride		
Run / Own A Team		

Use a chart like this one to evaluate the pluses and minuses of your series options, considering the present stage of your career.

you've run out of money. The sad thing is that most racers get caught up in the disease called racing and don't have that self-discipline. But, at least it's an option, whereas if you've signed a contract with a team, you're committed.

One last advantage is that you should have more control over the people on your team than when renting a ride. This should help in surrounding yourself with the right people.

When to Step Up

Perhaps one of the most difficult decisions you may face in your career is when to move up the ladder to the next level of race series. That's a good problem to have, since if you have to make that decision, at least you have the option of moving up. Some drivers won't have that option due to budget challenges.

So, when do you move up? Let's assume that you did not win the championship in the series in which you're now competing. Let's say you finished fifth in the championship, even though you showed well, had a few podium finishes, and led two races before a DNF in one race and fell back to fourth in the other. Should you move up to the next level, or go back and try to win the championship?

We wish it was easy to answer this question. It isn't. But here are some factors to consider. Was this your first season in that series? If so, it can't hurt to do it for another season. If it was your second or third season in the series, you don't want to make a career out of one series, so it may be time to move on.

If instead of just having had some podium finishes, you won a race, then perhaps you should move on. If you haven't won a race in a series and you have time, stay until you have won; prove that you can win at a level before moving on. Too many drivers feel that they need to move too quickly, and because of that they don't learn how to win. You may have won in the other series' in the past, but you need to know that you can win at the next level.

We want to stress this point because it's so important. You need to learn how to win before moving up too quickly. You may say you know how to win if you have the right equipment, but that's part of what we're talking about. You need to know you can get yourself in the right equipment. You need to know you *have* won, not just that you *can* win.

SPEED SECRET #9
Learn how to win before moving on to another series.

This is the main reason we stress not moving too quickly to the next level: it's important to be successful at one level before moving to the next. After all, if you can't win in the series you're in now, what makes you think you can win at the next one? Winning is what we're after. Just participating is not something that you can build a career around.

Of course, you can stay in a development series too long, as well. If you become a permanent resident of the series, that's too long. A warning sign: if you are personal friends with the series personnel, you've been there too long.

Another factor to consider: have you learned everything you can from this series? If so, perhaps it's time to move up, even if you haven't won. Be honest, though. Many drivers will say they've learned everything they can, using that as the reason for moving on, only to find themselves struggling at the next level. If they had been honest with themselves and stayed until they had learned everything they could, they might have been able to avoid the struggle at the more expensive and higher profile series.

If you have learned everything you're going to learn (at least almost everything, as it's impossible to ever learn everything), don't waste your time. Unless you feel that you can go back and totally dominate the series with your knowledge, move on. Until you're at the very top of the ladder (in NASCAR, IRL/Indy car, Grand-Am/ALMS, or F1), your goal in every step of the way should be to learn more in order to develop as a driver. If you've gotten most of what you're ever going to get from a series, move to a series where you can learn more.

Racing should always be just a little uncomfortable; it should be a stretch. When driving, if you're always comfortable, you're probably not driving at the limit. Same thing applies to your career. If you're comfortable in a series, then you're probably not learning a lot. If it's a stretch for you to compete at your current level, then you are definitely learning.

Of course, if you're too uncomfortable, you're probably in that brain-overload situation. In this position, you are not learning much, you're not having much fun, and you're bound to lose motivation over time. In that case, you're probably better off taking a step backwards.

What about taking a step backwards—stepping back a series for financial or other reasons? If you do so, you had better dominate the series. If you do it and are then just mediocre, your career could lose steam. Be very careful about stepping back, but if it's the right thing to do, you must have the guts to do it and to defend your decision.

Momentum is another factor. If you've won or shown very well in a series, moved to the next series and done the same thing, then your career has some momentum. It's difficult to say for sure when a career has momentum, but if you pay close attention to what's being said and what's going on in that level of the sport, you should be able to tell. Of course, being as close to your career as you are, it's difficult to be objective or honest about it. Perhaps there are people who know you well whom you trust to ask for advice.

You need to be realistic about what your abilities are, what your next step toward success is going to be, and what resources you have. Just about anyone can step into a series and compete. But not many can be competitive. If your goal is to build a career, you need to do more than just show up and compete. You need to compete for wins. You need to run at the front. You need to be a factor. If you're moving up for the sake of saying you've driven at that level, be honest with yourself about your career. Racers don't drive to say they do it. They race to win because doing anything else is unthinkable.

SPEED SECRET #10

There's a difference between competing and being competitive. Be competitive if you want a racing career.

What are your objectives? Are you truly trying to develop a career, or do you just want to be there? If your goal is to just say you've competed at a certain level and you're happy being somewhere in the pack, that's okay as long as you're honest and up-front with yourself about that. But if your only goal is to make a career and get to the next level, then your focus is going to be different. It should be on making the maximum impact on the racing world and dominating a series.

This is another critical factor in your decision making. You will always do more for your career by dominating a lower level series than by just participating in a higher level series. (See our previous discussions about deciding when to move on once you've had a dominant season.)

SPEED SECRET #11
Put yourself in position to dominate a series.

Your career is somewhere along this spectrum, from the beginning stages where developing your skills is the most important priority, to the point in your career where your only focus is on winning. Understanding where you are at all times will help when making career decisions.

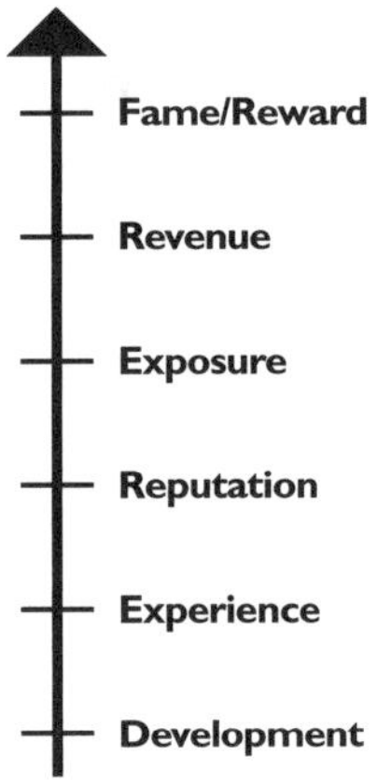

If you want to make it based on your abilities behind the wheel and not on your ability to bring money to a team, you must do more than win a race or two and the championship. You need to dominate. Every year, every series championship is won by some driver. How many of those champions can you name a year later? Few, we bet. The names you and team owners remember are of the drivers who have done more than just won a season championship. When Paul Tracy won the Indy Lights championship, he set a new record for the number of wins in a season. Then Greg Moore beat that record. Team owners remembered that. You need to dominate a series to be anywhere near guaranteed a chance, based solely on your driving talent, to move up.

There are things you can do that can help you reach a level of dominance and get yourself noticed. To do it, all you need is one of the best cars, best teams, and best budgets to operate with, and to be one of the most talented drivers. If these goals seem self-evident or overwhelming, step back and reassess you career chances. This is what being a paid professional requires. Get the money, the parts, and the tuning you need to make your car competitive. The top drivers in your series are doing this. Find out how and do the same. Study their technique, work with your driving coach or mentor to equal their performance, and take them on. If you can't do it at one level, how will you be able to do it in a more competitive series?

In the end, your options to move up may hinge on financial issues. Sometimes you may find the budget to move up, even when you're not fully prepared. What are you going to do, say no to the budget? Doubtful, even if that would be the smart decision. In that case, it would be best if you honestly assessed what you need to be more prepared in, and made that part of your program for the season.

The opposing situation is if it's time to move up, but you don't have the budget to do so. Some people—smart people—will tell you to have the budget for one level higher than you are racing. Those resources should be very helpful to your efforts to dominate the level below. Should you move up if you don't have the best budget? No. You're better off dominating a lower level series than running mid-pack at a higher level.

One-Off Rides

Every now and then, a driver gets the opportunity to do a one-off—a one-race deal to drive something different. If you get this opportunity, should you take it? That depends.

First of all, many one-offs turn into full season deals, so they are definitely worth chasing after. How do you get one? By getting your name out there, by talking to teams, by doing whatever it takes to find one.

Other than the opportunity of the one-off turning into a full season deal, it is a great way to gain some experience. It is also a good way of testing out a team, car, or series to see if it's a good fit for you. If you can check the team, car, or series out in a one-off deal, you can make a better informed decision before moving in that direction for the next season.

The question is: "Should you drive anything?" Depending on where you are in your career, if someone offers you a one-off ride for free, you will probably want to take it no matter what. But there are free rides you should turn down. There are two main reasons for turning down a free ride, with safety being number one. Before taking a ride, do your homework and check out the car, be honest and very critical, and make sure it is safe. The second reason is if the ride is going to do more harm to your career than good. Of course, this is a difficult one to determine beforehand, and an easy one to look back on and say it was good or bad. If it doesn't feel good, it probably isn't. If it seems to be too good to be true, it probably is. There are many one-offs that end up doing more harm then good, and again, you have to determine whether it will damage your career rather than further it. We've seen far too many one-offs do more to hurt a driver's career than we've seen one-offs help. The one-off ride was a poorly prepared car, and the results did not showcase the driver's abilities. In fact, it made him look bad. Or, the one-off was with a team that had a very poor business reputation, which then fell on to the driver. Think about it long and hard before jumping at something that initially looks like a great opportunity.

Scholarship Shootouts, Tryouts, Tests

Opportunity. That is what a scholarship shootout, or a team tryout/test is. It could be what makes your career take off, or it could just be a great opportunity to learn and develop as a driver.

So, how do you get the opportunity in the first place? How do you get invited? If it's a formal scholarship program, such as the Red Bull Driver Search, the Skip Barber Karting Scholarship, or the Jim Russell Racing School scholarship, you need to qualify first. That may be just a matter of being successful in other forms of motorsport—that's all! Most of these programs are looking for drivers who have proven themselves to be successful already. You must have a record of winning races and/or championships even to get noticed. Then, you will need to go through some form of filter to qualify for the finals.

It's important to understand the motivation for any of these companies to provide these scholarship programs. While it would be nice to say that their reasons were only altruistic, that's the not the whole story. Yes, they are racing people and they want to see young drivers succeed—there is some philanthropy involved. But what they most care about is the promotional value that comes from the program. They care about the amount of media coverage they get. They care about being able to brag about the driver who won their scholarship and then went on to bigger and greater things. Ultimately, they care about generating more business from it, and there is absolutely nothing wrong with that. They are doing something for themselves by providing an opportunity for you. The most important thing to realize, though, is the motivation behind the program. It will make you better prepared to make a good impression on the people making the selection.

With that in mind, it's understandable that most of the scholarships out there are focused on taking a driver who is already very talented and giving him more. Rarely do they intend to take a driver who has raw, undeveloped potential and help to turn it into a winning package. They usually intend to take a winner and piggyback on that driver's success in the future.

Now, a test or tryout for a team may be a little different, but ultimately they are looking for a driver who can win immediately, as well. They don't want to wait a year or two for a driver to fully develop; they can't afford that.

So, given all that background, let's assume you get an invite to a test or shootout. You're going to get a day or two in a car to prove what you can provide to the company or team. How should you approach it? Should you be a little on the conservative side or go all out? Should you risk throwing the car off the track and maybe even crashing it to get the last 10th of a second out of it? Or should you prove yourself to be a good, solid driver who never makes a mistake?

We know what you're thinking. Yes, to both! Be a solid driver who never makes a mistake, but get that last 10th out of the car, too. Well, that's great, but sometimes it's not possible to take both the conservative and go-for-broke approach. So, if you had to choose just one, which would it be?

We've never heard a team or shootout selection committee make a comment about a driver like, "Remember Johnny? He wasn't the fastest driver we've ever tested, but he sure was consistent." That never happens. In fact, if Johnny was not very fast but was consistent, there's a much better chance the committee wouldn't even remember his name.

However, we have heard people say, even months or years later, "Remember Tommy? Man, was he fast! He threw the car off the track a couple of times, but what speed!" People in racing—at least the serious ones—know that it's much easier to dial a driver down than it is to dial one up. They would rather take a driver who is very fast and help him become more consistent and error-free than the other way around.

SPEED SECRET #12

If you have one opportunity to strut your stuff—your speed—take it.

Do your best to determine what the team or company is looking for, and how much risk it can afford for you to take. There are drivers who have lost any chance of getting an opportunity by crashing a car. Ask the team right upfront what it is looking for—speed, feedback, consistency? Of course, many times the team will tell you one thing, but deep down it is looking for something else. In other words, if someone else is faster than you, he'll probably get the ride.

Which brings up another good question: is there any pressure when you get a chance to test? It all depends on how you look at it. You can look at it as the one and only chance you'll ever have, the opportunity of a lifetime, and if you screw it up you've screwed up your entire life. Yes, that will generate a little pressure! Or, you can look at it as an opportunity to drive a race car, and no matter what happens, you will have gained more experience and be better prepared for the other opportunities that come along. Guess which approach is most likely to help you the most in handling the pressure?

A shootout or test is an opportunity for you to learn, and if things work out the right way, you may get another one. Our advice is to take that attitude, and the chances of you performing well enough to win will improve. The best way to deal with pressure is not to build it in the first place, and then just perform your best.

A word of warning regarding feedback on the car's setup is appropriate here. There are teams that will purposely ask you to make a few laps to get a read on the setup change they have just made. They may or may not tell you what exactly they've changed, with the objective of seeing how well you sense the change and can communicate it back to them. Worse still, they may tell you they did something to the car when, in fact, they have done nothing to it. Imagine what they think if you go out, do a few laps, come in, and make up something just to convince them that you can provide good feedback. It happens.

SPEED SECRET #13

Always be totally honest and accurate with what you felt or did not feel with a chassis change.

There is absolutely nothing wrong with telling a team that you did not notice any difference with a change. The team may have done nothing to the car, or it may have made a change that it knows will be practically impossible to feel. It may be testing you in more ways than you think. And as you probably know, there are setup changes that have little to no effect on what you will feel. Be honest.

Dress and present yourself professionally. That means no jeans, no T-shirts, and get a fresh haircut. Look in the mirror and ask yourself if a company would want to spend millions of dollars on you. Do you look the part?

Prepare, bring, and present a marketing/promotional package. Don't have one? Have it made—by a pro or by you. And then present one to each and every judge, media person, official, or key team member involved with the program. (You may be surprised who the main influence is when selecting a driver for a team. The team owner or manager may leave that decision to the mechanics.)

If it's a scholarship shootout, research as much as possible on how it is conducted. Is it strictly based on your on-track performance? If so, is that just the quickest lap time, or do consistency, lack of errors, and feedback on chassis setup play a role in the decision? How many laps or sessions will you most likely get? If there's more to it than on-track performance, what? Do you have to make a presentation to the judges? Are there mock media interviews? Are you interviewed by the judges about your goals? You may be able to ask another driver who has been through it in the past for some advice.

Research all the available information on the company behind the scholarship. Review every piece of information on its website, and do a search on the web. Be prepared to sound somewhat knowledgeable about the company, which could be supporting your racing career. If nothing else, it demonstrates your willingness to work with and your commitment to the company.

Obviously, get as much information as you can about the cars and track you'll be driving. Talk to other drivers who have driven the car or track. Be as prepared as possible.

Make sure you know what your goals are for the shootout and your future. You could be asked this. If you are slightly vague about what your goals are and how you intend to achieve them, that doesn't look good. You should have a five-year career plan written out. You don't have to present it to the judges or team, but you better have it mapped out in your head, and the best way to do that is by writing it out. As with the marketing/promotional materials, you can hire a pro or do it yourself.

Have a hook, something that separates you from all the rest of the young, fast drivers. (We'll cover this in more detail later in the book.) For example, capitalize on a major accomplishment in another sport or activity, a skill or talent that other drivers don't have, a contact or relationship with someone of importance, or anything else that singles you out. Think: "If it came down to me and two other drivers and all of our on-track performances were identical, why would they pick me?" Once you've identified and developed your hook, communicate it to the judges or team through your marketing/promotional materials and in person.

Be ready with at least three key messages that you would like to say if you were interviewed on the victory podium. Don't wait until you're there to figure it out. Prepare them and practice presenting them over and over again. That way, when you're asked during the shootout—whether mock or for real—you'll feel confident and comfortable since you're ready and prepared. Also, you will have bought yourself some time to think about other comments while saying what you have already prepared.

Be yourself. If you have a personality, let it show. In fact, be prepared to turn up the volume on it a little if you're naturally quiet and reserved. People, and more importantly, sponsors, love drivers with personalities, especially if it's a well-defined part of your package as a driver.

Focus on your performance, not on the competition, the result, or what could or couldn't happen. There is only one thing you can control, and that's you. You can't control your competition. You can't control the result or decision the judges make. You can influence the judges' decision, but only by performing at your best. Focus on the act of driving and on what you do best in and out of the car.

Drive the car as quickly as you can. Remember the simple job description for a professional race driver: drive the car at the limit, no more no less.

Work at developing a relationship with the mechanic(s) and the team. Often, the mechanics have more influence on your performance then you can ever imagine. They may be able to lobby to see you in another car, perform some subtle changes to make the car work better, or even provide some driving insights that they've picked up from other drivers.

If the shootout provides driving instructors, get the most out of them. Many will not go out of their way to do more than they are paid to do. However, if you ask for their advice and help, they will respect you for seeking it and give you more information. They may take you under their wing, and even put a vote in for you.

At a shootout, be careful not to hang out too closely with other drivers, even if they're close friends. Who knows, if your friend is not well-liked by the judges, you may be painted with the same brush. Be yourself. And don't give away your secrets to other drivers. Remember, this is a competition.

Don't come out and blame the car for your lack of speed. Yes, it's impossible for all cars to perform identically, and it's possible your car is worse than the others. However, most times it is not the car, it's the driver's inability to adapt to the car—that means you. Sorry, but it's a fact. If you feel your car is not performing well, focus on adapting your driving to overcome the problem. Okay, you should certainly mention your challenge, but do it politely, quietly, and don't blame, sulk, whine, or whinge. Most judges have the experience to recognize a car that is not performing, and they will actually give you extra points for dealing with it in a mature manner.

However, do not ignore a problem with your car; make sure you communicate any problems you have. Part of being a professional race driver is conveying issues with your car in a constructive manner.

Chapter 6

Business

The days of a race driver having to focus only on driving the car are long gone. Some would say they never existed, as drivers have always had to work the business side of the sport to stay in it for any length of time. But for sure, this side is more important now than ever before.

The fact is, *you* are a business, not just a race driver. The sooner you recognize this fact and turn it to your advantage, the better your career will be.

SPEED SECRET #14

The sooner you begin operating like a business, with proper planning and financial control, the better your chances are of a career as a professional race driver.

So, you're a business. What is your business? You may say your business is, "You as a race driver," and that the business is, "You driving race cars." Technically, you're correct. However, if all there is to your business is you driving, that's not much. You need more. Why? Because there are many drivers out there, and a lot of them have talent just like you.

So, what differentiates you from rest? Why would someone hire you to drive his car? What do you bring to the table?

For example, part of what set Ross apart from other drivers is his ability to coach other drivers. During the years when he was really focused on finding a paid ride, that was what differentiated him from others in the field, and he got paid to drive because he brought more to the table than just his driving abilities.

The more you can think of yourself as a product or service, the better you'll be. If you think that a team or a sponsor would buy you, why? If not, why not? Ask yourself these questions and then plan to make yourself more saleable.

We also would suggest you think about what your personal values are. What are you willing to do to make it as a race driver? Be honest with yourself. It doesn't matter what the answer is, and you don't have to share it with anyone but yourself. But it is important that you know what it is you're willing to do and what values you represent. John Force, a multiple world champion drag racer, spent his early years driving his own rig, sleeping in it, and cutting deals on the road to fund his next tank of gas. When he took his crew to a motel, he slept in the bathtub and they separated the mattresses from the box springs to sleep four in

Are you a race driver or businessperson? Both, right? Learning to operate like a business may be a little foreign or unappealing to you, but it can give you an edge on the competition off the track.

separate "beds." He lived a hand-to-mouth, deal-to-deal existence for years. And now he's a racing legend. Do you have that commitment, that willingness, to lay everything on the line?

Agents/Managers

A question we're often asked is, "Do I need a manager or agent?" This is a tough question to answer, mostly because we believe there are more bad managers/agents out there than there are good ones.

First, let's look at what a good manager or agent can do for you. A manager who has been around the sport for quite a while will have many contacts with teams, series personnel, and potential sponsors. He will be able to introduce you to these people, and get you "in the know" in much less time than you could ever do yourself. If he's a good one, he will come with credibility and have the ability to walk up to the key players in the sport and represent you.

A good manager will also negotiate any agreements with teams or sponsors and look after your best interests, while also making sure the team or sponsor feels good about the relationship. In an ideal situation, he will have examples of other agreements that have worked for other drivers, teams, and sponsors.

The downside of managers and agents is that they often put their own interests ahead of yours. We've seen too many over-promise and under-deliver on a driver's behalf. They promise a sponsor, for example, that the driver will make a certain number of appearances for them, even though the driver could never fulfill that promise. The manager doesn't care all that much; he got the deal done, and it's the driver who ultimately looks bad in the end. By that point, the manager figures he'll be onto another deal.

Bad managers hurt drivers' reputations more than they could ever help. Good managers provide a lot of value.

Our advice is to be very careful when contracting with a manager or agent. Ask around to see what kind of reputation he has. Get and check references. We've met managers who gave us a couple of references who said good things about him, only to ask around a bit more and find some horror stories about him. If we hadn't been thorough, the driver considering this manager could have found himself in a bad situation. In this instance, having an experienced mentor who you can ask for advice is a big advantage. If the mentor has been around the sport for a long time, there's a good chance he has a lot of contacts and can really check out someone you're considering as a manager.

It's important to keep in mind that it is your reputation that a manager will be playing with. The only way you can control your reputation 100 percent is to do all your own management. While this may not be what you want or the best way, it is the only way to make sure you maintain a reputation for delivering on your promises.

Make sure that you have approved any and all contracts and promises made to a team or sponsor before they are finalized. And you need that in writing with your manager. Make sure he cannot promise or contract anything without your prior knowledge and approval. If he's honest, he should have nothing to fear by signing such an agreement with you. This is one time where you will definitely need a lawyer to make sure your contract protects you. Spend the time and money to make sure it is done right the first time. (The good news is that once you have it, you will be able to use it for many years with other managers and agents.)

SPEED SECRET #15

Take your time with contracts and agreements. This is one place you don't want to be fast.

Again, make sure you maintain control of any relationship of this type, and you have control over your manager. Without that control, you may have more headaches down the road than you can imagine.

In the end, any manager (or any other consultant) you choose to work with must have the same core values, morals, and ethics as you do, otherwise the arrangement will end in problems. A manager must believe in treating people and business situations the same way you do. You need to know he will work with people in the same manner and with the same level of commitment as you would. Without the same core values, you can be sure that things will not work out, either between the two of you or between you and the company or team with which he's negotiated a contract.

Administration

More race drivers get themselves into financial difficulties than any other business problem. The cause? Their passion? No, their addiction to racing. As you know, this sport can be almost like an addiction, in that once you have it, you can't kick it. And that leads to financial problems, just like someone who is addicted to drugs spending every last dime he has to feed his habit.

The sooner you put some financial systems in place, the easier it will be to control your addiction.

For example, developing a detailed budget for each season—right down to the last dollar—and then keeping track of every expenditure along the way will help provide some needed discipline. Most financial problems seem to happen when a driver loses sight of how much has been spent in relation to what was planned. Early in the season, when you consider a budget for the whole season, it may seem like you have plenty to work with. But overspending by any amount at all means you're going to run out of money before the end of the season. The only way for that not to happen is if you had over-budgeted, but that is extremely unlikely. Things rarely work as planned throughout a whole season, and in racing, virtually every unforeseen event costs money—crashes, broken parts, personnel changes, etc. Prices in the world tend to rise, not fall. Watch your dollars closely throughout the season so you can field a good effort all season long. From the very first cost overrun, get your finances back in balance right away.

Most times, when someone has overspent, he doesn't even know it until it's too late. By the time he realizes it, he's over-extended, and then has a tough time getting back on the financial track. If he had kept better track of expenditures, they would have been easier to control.

So, if you do nothing else, make sure you have a detailed budget going into each season, know exactly what you have to spend, and then track your spending in real time. Do not wait until a month later to find out how much you actually spent on a race event. Use a simple accounting program, track it with credit card statements, or even pay in cash if that's what it takes to stay disciplined.

Once a driver has a bad reputation for not paying a bill on time, it takes a long time for that to go away. And the racing community is a small one. Word gets around very quickly about people who do not pay bills or live up to promises.

Doing Business

Like any business, you will need some materials. For starters, you absolutely need to have business cards that represent you well. Take a bit of time to make sure they look good and characterize you the way you want to be seen. You know what they say about first impressions, and often your business card is the first tangible thing somebody sees that represents you.

The same applies to letterhead and envelopes. While these are not as important as they once were, due to the preference for e-mail now, there are times when you will need to use them. Again, make sure they present the professional image. Our suggestion is to go for simplicity over trick, elaborate designs. Make sure the text and any logo, design, or layout are easy to read.

One thing for sure is that, as a race driver, you will travel a lot! What's surprising is how many drivers there are who do not take advantage of the only real benefit of flying that often. The sooner you begin collecting frequent flyer points, the better off you'll be. There will come a time when your points will cover a flight to meet with a prospective sponsor or team, allowing you to put the money you saved toward your racing costs. You're going to travel a lot, so you might as well get some additional benefits from it.

There is one other thing you need to take advantage of when flying, and that's meeting people. While we would never suggest harassing the people, if you can strike up a conversation with someone sitting next to you on a plane, you never know where that may lead. Many complete strangers have become strong supporters (financially and otherwise) for race drivers just because the driver made the effort, and then showed true enthusiasm for what he's doing. If you love what you're doing, don't be afraid to tell other people about it. For this reason, consider your personal presentation (particularly how you dress) while flying. It would be a shame if you sat next to a company CEO (you would be surprised how many successful business executives fly in economy class), and you were dressed in a way that did not represent you very well.

As to meeting people, here's another thing to keep in mind. Early in your career, you may actually make a huge contact, one so big it would be your dream to get sponsorship from his company. At that point, your own modesty or fear that he thinks you're a bigger deal than you are, may cause you to downplay your own ability or feel guilty that maybe you're misleading them. The drivers who make it in this world—people who make it big in any business—never sell themselves short. Either you believe in yourself or you don't. If you do, you can make it. If you don't, you almost surely will not. You have to be willing to drive your heart out for any sponsor that will give you money, and that's all they can ask.

Sell yourself as a professional driver. Believe that you're worth it, and other people will too. That attitude has to underlie every conversation you have about racing. Passion and enthusiasm are contagious.

SPEED SECRET #16

Being a professional race driver is not a part-time job. Always dress and act like a pro, and you will increase your chances of being a pro.

Play the part of a professional at all times. Be prepared to talk to anyone and everyone about what you do and where you're going. If you're not prepared, you're not in the business of being a race driver.

Like every successful business, you will need some way to budget, track, and control what you spend, whether it's your money or someone else's. The sooner you learn how to develop an operating budget using a spreadsheet (and perhaps later use some form of accounting program), the closer to being a professional race driver you will be.

We would suggest having both a lawyer and an accountant on hand as consultants. You may wonder if you'll really need them (especially a lawyer) but believe us, you will. At least, we hope you will desperately need them. If you're active as a driver and making some money, you will need these consultants in your business.

It's relatively easy these days to find a standard contract template to modify in order to suit your situation. But contract terms are subject to legal constructions of words and phrases that often differ from their day-to-day meaning. There may also be desirable provisions that the template you find does not include. Only a lawyer can guide you through a contract's legal language and ensure that the contract best reflects your interests. Take the time and money and invest both into getting your agreements checked over by a lawyer.

The same can be said for accountants. We're not suggesting you have to have one full-time on staff, but it's likely you will need an accountant two or three times a year. For that reason alone, you should have one lined up and ready to go to help you with your financial needs.

You don't have to hire the biggest firm in town, just someone competent. Maybe there's a place for a "Barbara Smith, Attorney at Law" or "Fred Nelson, CPA" sticker on your fender. Barter. Negotiate. Every person in your life is a potential supporter. Odds are pretty good that a race driver will be one of your accountant's or attorney's more interesting clients. These are well-connected professions. Get them to come to a race and bring some friends. You get the idea. As soon as you start seeing yourself as an opportunity for others, the more quickly your race business will grow.

When is a contract unnecessary between you and a team or sponsor? That's a trick question, because you always need a contract. We sometimes hear drivers say that they didn't think they needed one because they were dealing with a friend. That comment is usually made around the time when that friendship ended, and the arguing over who was supposed to do what and where and when began. Always get the details in writing. Remember, in order to make sure you're on the same page, you actually need a page.

Chapter 7

Teams

Working with a Team

Each of the previous *Speed Secrets* books has taken a different perspective on how important it is to build your team. By that we mean being the team leader, motivating the entire team, and being the one the team rallies behind. We call this the Schumacher effect, since Michael may be the very best at this key trait and skill.

We won't rehash the topics here that were covered in those past books (it may be worth re-reading those sections though). What we will discuss specifically is how to work with a teammate. At some point in your career you will most likely have one or more drivers on the same team with you. Let's look at the issues you will need to deal with should this be the case.

The first question is if you should work together and share information with your teammate. If so, how should you go about doing that? Some drivers consider a teammate as the very first driver they must beat, and therefore don't give him any information. Other drivers feel that they can benefit by being open with their teammate, and so share everything they have. Some teams insist on their drivers sharing, while others discourage it.

If the decision of whether to share information with a teammate is your decision and not the team's, then we believe it is something of a moral decision, and one that only you can make. You have to feel comfortable with it. If you decide to do everything you can to mess up your teammate in an attempt to gain the advantage, that's something that you need to feel good about. On the other hand, if you give everything away to your teammate and he ends up beating you, how are you going to feel?

An approach you can take is this: be willing to share any information with your teammate that he asks for, and expect and ask for the same in return. Then, make sure you ask for more from him than he does from you. In fact, dig as deep as you can. Learn by asking to share data, from asking questions about driving techniques, and from listening to everything said in team debriefs. Look to gain an advantage, but in a completely fair manner, and let the best (prepared) driver win.

Racing has always been, and will always be, a team sport, no matter how isolated and alone you are in the car on the track. The more team-building you do, the more successful you will be.

SPEED SECRET #17
Turn every teammate situation into an advantage.

A quick word on team loyalty. There are opposing forces you need to balance. Being loyal, and building a reputation for being an honest, trustworthy person, will greatly increase your chances of a career in racing. If you treat people and teams like their only purpose in life is to be your stepping stones on your way to the top, you won't have many people supporting you for long. On the other hand, you should always keep in mind that there may be a better opportunity or person to help you reach your goals. Some drivers are too loyal and their careers suffer because they failed to take advantage of someone or some team that is better. They have often become too friendly or emotionally attached to the people on the team.

As we said, these are obviously opposing forces you need to balance. Too far in either direction will prevent your career from blossoming as it should.

The ideal situation—and the perfect balance—is if you can build such a mutually respectful relationship with your existing team that even it will push you to leave for a better opportunity. If you've done your team-building job, the members will hate to see you leave, but will wish you good luck as they encourage you to take the next step.

SPEED SECRET #18

Build your team relationship to the point where it will encourage you to find the best opportunity for yourself, and even help you find it.

Selecting a Team

In Chapter 5 we began the discussion of choosing a team to rent-a-ride with, but now let's get a little more detailed. If a team selects you, it's a little different, but some of this will also apply to the situation where you have two offers to drive—two teams fighting over your services.

Start by considering a team's reputation. Of course, that covers many areas, such as its results, ease of working relationship, financial dealings, and trustworthiness.

Results are pretty easy to determine, although you should also consider how and where the team got the results. Some teams have gained a great reputation of being able to win championships in one level of the sport, but when they move to another series, they struggle. Success at one level does not guarantee it at another level. However, there are some teams that seem to be able to win at every level and in every series in which they compete. These are teams you want to run with.

When considering reputation, also look at whether the team is on its way up, or on its way down. Most teams, even Ferrari, Williams,

McLaren, Penske, Ganassi, Hendrick, and Roush, have their ups and downs (it's cyclical). Sometimes it's caused by changing personnel, or just finding the right combination of people; sometimes it's due to technical reasons; and other times it's a matter of how strong the team's motivation is. The point is, there are teams on their way up the cycle and others are on their way down. Guess where you want to join?

Of course, this is not an easy thing to determine. It's not something you can just ask the team owner, although doing so may give you some insight. Looking at past and current results, as well as talking to other people in the sport (especially series personnel), may help you in determining this important factor.

Some of the other considerations, such as the team's financial strength and its ability to manage your money and work with you, are even more difficult to ascertain. You need to do some homework. You should talk to knowledgeable people, particularly drivers who have run with that team in the past. Ask a lot of questions, of others and of the team itself. If you're the one spending the money, don't be afraid to dig deep. It's likely to be a fair amount of money, so take your time and do things right up front. If you don't, you'll regret it later.

Determine the team's motivation. Is it to win championships, help young drivers, make money, give the owner an ego boost, or what? None of these reasons are necessarily exclusive, as it's likely there will be some overlap, but there is usually one main motivation for the team. We're not even suggesting that one reason is any better than another, but it should match your objectives.

For example, if the team's existence is really a way to boost the owner's ego by getting his name mentioned in the media a lot, then that may not fit your objectives if your goal is to maximize the coverage you get as a result of your performance. It would most likely not be a good a fit.

Is the team in this for the money? Let's hope so, at least to some point. If the team is not in it to be profitable, there's a better chance that it will struggle financially at some point during the season, causing your results to suffer. If the team owner tells you he is not in it for the money, and it doesn't matter if he makes any, be concerned. Even if the team owner has all the money in the world, it matters.

There's a reason he has that much money; he's not stupid about the way he spends it. If the race team begins costing him too much money, he will cut back. If you've been relying on his support and it goes away, you will suffer.

We're not saying that there are no teams that are willing to support your program to some extent. To some, making money is not the priority; their real motivation may be helping drivers. There are team owners who have driver development as a motivation. If you can find one, good for you. But be careful; don't automatically think you have a team owner with this motivation when you really don't. Again, that's why you need to do your homework and dig for the real motivation behind the team. Then see if it's a good fit for you and your program.

Once you know what the team's motivation is, your next step is to find out how keen it is to reach your goals. If your goal is to win the championship or die while the team is okay with just participating in the series, then it's not a good match. Can you step up its motivation? Can you help it become a winning team? While that can and has happened (look at what Michael Schumacher did, first with Benetton and then with Ferrari), it's rare in the junior formula ranks. If the team isn't a winner, just realize it will be a challenge to turn it into one. Again, we're not saying you can't do it. We're just saying it is not easy and you need to factor that into your decision of which team you select.

The big question becomes: What is the team willing to do to help you win?

Also consider how you fit in the team. How much importance does the team put on having fun? How ethical is it? Will it push the rules to win? How business-like is it? How committed is it? And how do these attributes mesh with yours? There is no right or wrong answer to any of these questions. It only matters that it's a good fit.

How well staffed is the team and how qualified are the staff members? We've seen teams in the junior formula ranks that have more people than some IRL teams, yet that don't win because of their abilities. We've also seen the opposite—one-man teams that kick butt. Others seem to have the perfect number of qualified people, and yet they still don't win. These are not teams. As in any sport, sometimes the very best people just don't combine well to make a great team.

What is the team's level of resources? By that we mean does it have the financial strength to quickly cover some unexpected problem (should that be needed)? Or will it have to cut into your budget, and perhaps sacrifice something that may affect the results? If the team is on the financial ragged edge of survival, do you want to take that chance? Ross once coached a driver whose last couple of races of the season were borderline dangerous. (The team had to cut so many corners on car prep because of the lack of money.) The team had not been prepared for any unexpected cost, which is the one thing you can expect in racing, during the season. Consider whether the team has the financial strength to deal with them.

Will you have a teammate with the team in question? That may or may not be a good thing, but it's something you need to consider. Teammates can be a distraction, or they can help you become better (see previous chapter). If the team does have multiple drivers, are there any written or unwritten rules as to who gets preferential treatment? Even if there are no written, or agreed-upon, driver preferences at the beginning of a season, there will always—and we mean always—end up being one driver who gets better treatment than the other(s). Of course, this has more to do with human nature than anything else. If one driver shows more commitment to the team, consistently gets better results, or treats the people on the team better than the others, he will eventually get better treatment by the team, whether the members realize they are doing this or not. Again, it's human nature.

If you're considering joining a team in which you will have a teammate, can you "take control" of the team? Can you be seen as the leader? Can you get the preferential treatment? If not, you may be better off finding another team. This is a bigger deal than it appears, so think about it. If you want to come in second, don't worry about being your team leader. If you want to win, you must be the team leader. Unless you're in the stage of your career where learning from a more experienced teammate may be helpful, if you're not sure you can be the leader within a team, look elsewhere.

This leads right into a sensitive issue that must be considered if the team owner or a family member drives for the team. This could be considered a conflict of interest, although it is not always the case. If the team owner, or his family member, drives for the team, no matter how fairly you are treated, you will question your treatment at some point. It's human nature to look for something to blame when things are not going the way you want. If there is a family member in the team, you're bound to perceive some unfairness. Our experience is that most team owners in this situation are more than fair. In fact, they often give the edge to the customer (you), but there are always conflicts between perception and reality.

To avoid this situation you need to be contractually covered for every possible situation that could ever come up. But most importantly, you need to feel 100 percent confident with the people you're dealing with. If you don't feel you can fully trust the team owner to do what is right, then no contract in the world will make it work. If the team owner or his family member is a driver in the team, be careful and protect yourself.

An obvious consideration in your team selection process has to be the equipment. If you're looking at a series where multiple chassis or engine packages are available, you had better be sure you're driving the best package. That decision is more difficult than it appears, as proven by the number of extremely experienced and knowledgeable teams that have ended up running less-than-competitive chassis/engine packages; they made a bad decision as to which would be the most competitive. You need to evaluate this decision, and be totally convinced that the package you'll be driving is the very best.

The equipment factor is not restricted to just the car, although that is obviously the most important. Especially if you have sponsors, though, the team's transporter and hospitality options, as well as the team's shop, are other factors to consider. In the end, once you're convinced the team will be able to give you the hardware—equipment, results, personnel, etc.—your values, goals, and passion (software) should fit the team you're considering. It needs to be a comfortable setting for you.

Once you've selected your team, the next step is to define what the common goals, objectives, and responsibilities are and ensure these are all spelled out in an agreement. It may seem obvious what the responsibilities are, but it rarely is. Who's going to arrange passes for your guests? Who's going to make sure media releases are sent out?

Who's going to clean your driving suit after a weekend? Who's responsible for sending in the entry forms?

Make sure you know exactly what you're getting for each dollar you spend. Some teams include everything in their deal, while others can nickel-and-dime you to death if you're not careful. That's why so many team budgets that are floated around the racing community mean little to nothing; you're rarely comparing apples to apples. Make sure you know who's covering entry fees (both season-long series and individual event fees), crew passes/credentials and wages, tires, engine rebuilds, consumables (gears, brake pads, fluids, etc.), transport fees, crew travel, driver travel, driver license fees, driver safety equipment, and the big one . . . crash damage.

Building/Operating Your Own Team

Rather than rent a ride with a team, you can also put together your own team and operate it yourself. In addition to the factors that we covered in Chapter 5, here are a few more for your consideration.

Ask yourself what your objectives are in running your own team. Are they to make a profit? Are they simply to give yourself more control? Is it to see your own name on the team's equipment and entry? Is it to benefit you or someone else? Are there reasons why you think this approach will help you win more often? If so, what are they?

Ask yourself if you want to be a team owner/manager or a driver. Which is most important? And even if driving is the priority, by how much? Is it a little or a lot more important?

When deciding between renting a ride with a team and starting and running your own, an important issue to consider is what you should do with the car and equipment when it's time to move up to the next level. More than one driver has had his career stunted by his inability to sell his current car in order to afford to move up to the next series level. If you've invested in a lot of equipment (trailer, tow vehicle, pit equipment, tools, and car) for one series and you want to move up to the next, will you need to sell this equipment before doing that? And if so, how difficult will that be? Will it delay your ability to move up, or at least restrict your flexibility to take advantage of an opportunity?

Having all their capital locked up in equipment that cannot be sold off in time has cost many drivers opportunities, which could have made a big impact on their careers. Think about it. Plan ahead.

Speaking of capital investment, what equipment will you need to invest in? Will you need to buy a car (or cars), trailer, tow vehicle, tools, and other equipment? Will you need to invest in a shop to work out of? If so, what else could that capital be used for? Could it be used to hire a marketing person to develop some sponsorship opportunities? What are you really investing in, a team with your name on it or your driving career?

An important piece of business advice was given to us once, and it went like this. Seven out of 10 problems in business are:

1. People
2. People
3. People
4. People
5. People
6. People
7. People

In other words, the biggest challenge in building and running a successful business is the people involved. (If you're wondering what the other three are, it doesn't matter. If you select and manage your people well, everything else is easy!)

Running a race team is no different. People are the key to a winning team. So, a critical challenge you will face when building and running your race team will be to select, attract, hire, and then manage the right people. If you think shaving that last 10th of a second off your lap time is difficult, wait until you select and manage your race team personnel!

Budgeting is obviously a crucial element to successfully operating your race team. If this has never been one of your personal strengths, perhaps running a team is not meant for you. In this book, we can't give you the details of how to build and maintain a budget for a team. A good rule of thumb, though, is to make your best estimate of the total cost for the season, then add another 50 percent. Unless you have a lot of experience budgeting for the specific series you're going to be running and you are good at managing to a budget, the plus-50 percent rule is a minimum.

If we had a last comment on running your own race team, it would be this. Every single team owner we've ever met has, at one time, underestimated what it took to build and run a successful team. Obviously it can be done—with great difficulty—but for every one of those teams that have succeeded, there are hundreds that have not. And every one of the successful teams has taken more work, more money, more great people . . . more of everything than the owner had originally planned.

SPEED SECRET #19

Wildly overestimate what it will take to build and run a race team, and you may actually be accurate.

If we're sounding like we're trying to discourage you from building and running your own race team, that's not entirely what we intend. We're just trying to be realistic. And since our focus here is on the driver—your driving abilities and career—it only makes sense that we would focus on what's best solely for the driver's performance. Operating a race team will take focus away from the development of your driving skills and from your career advancement. That is a fact.

Sure, there are advantages to building or operating your own race team. Most racers have no problem seeing the benefits, such as the control they have, the investment in equipment that they may be able to recoup someday, and so on. It's the challenges and downside of taking this approach that is so difficult for most racers, and that's why we are suggesting you take the time to consider the points we've made here. All of the advice delivered here comes from the same place as everything else in this book—from our own and many, many others' experience.

Chapter 8

Marketing

When we talk about marketing, we're talking about selling yourself. That covers branding, the promotion of you and your career, public relations, networking, and sponsorship. In this chapter, we'll cover a few basics and then get into more detail in the next few chapters.

SPEED SECRET #20

Marketing skills are every bit as important to your career as driving fast.

You Are a Brand

The first thing you need to understand is that you, as a driver, are a brand. When you think of a brand, you typically think of a logo or name, such as Apple, Coca-Cola, or BMW. But the logo and name are just a part of it. It's what that logo and name has to say that establishes its market presence.

Perhaps the best way to define a brand is how people describe you or your company, or in other words, what they say about you. How do people describe Apple? It's a computer company that is fun, simple, creative, and innovative right? They make it fun and easy to use their products. It's certainly a different brand from IBM, isn't it?

How does a company, or a driver, develop this brand? Apple has done much more than just advertise its logo. It makes products that are fun, colorful, interesting, modern, and creative. Apparently, Apple's working environment is similar to its image. Apple's brand is a reflection of how the company acts, and what it does. It's not just a logo in an ad.

How would people describe you behind your back? What words would they use? Are they the words you would want them to use? Would you like them to use other words? If so, which ones? What can you do to encourage people to use the words you would like them to use? How would you need to act or what would you need to do to encourage people to describe you the way you'd like them to?

For example, if you want your brand to be all about being the "all-American, small-town boy who makes good," how would you need to act around people? What would you need to do? Obviously, you'd need to act like the all-American, small-town boy, and you'd have to make good. But, in more detail, what would you look and act like and do to be described in that way? Possibly you would have to be hard-working, honest, humble, and focused.

What if people don't have any words to describe you? That may be worse than having the wrong ones. If people can't describe you in a few words, then you don't have a brand and you won't stand out from the crowd (all the other drivers trying to make it in this sport).

Think of a few drivers and define their brand. Buddy Rice . . . what's his brand? He has more of an *X Games* brand than the typical corporate America–type brand. What about Sam Hornish Jr., Dale Earnhardt Jr., Mark Weber, Danica Patrick? Each of these drivers has a brand. They are people that you can describe.

Can a brand be overused? You bet. If it's the same brand that many other drivers are using, then it's not much of a brand, and therefore

Ferrari	**Safety**
BMW	**Prestige**
Chevrolet	**Precision**
Volvo	**All American**
Rolls Royce	**Exotic**

A strong brand is easy to define. To prove it to yourself, quickly match these adjectives with these companies. These words describe what the company's brand means to you.

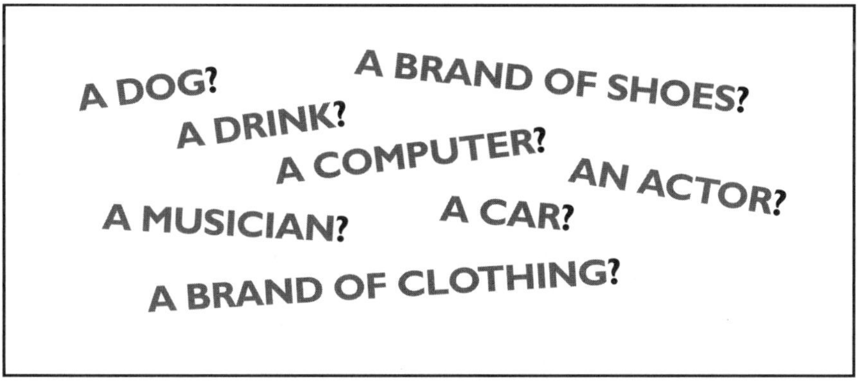

A good way to develop your brand is to match yourself with other well-known brands. Ask yourself, if you were a car, what kind of car would you be? A dog? A drink? A brand of clothing? A brand of shoes? A computer? A musician? An actor? Now ask yourself why? What is it about these brands that you identify with?

you'll blend in with the background. If you use the example we just referred to (the all-American, small-town boy who makes good), then you may not stand out. That's an overused brand. But if you grew up in the heart of NASCAR country and race sports cars in Europe, or you're a Martha's Vineyard–ite racing World of Outlaws sprint cars, that might make some news.

The bottom line is: you have a brand, no matter what. You can control it or allow it to control you. If you control it, you can use it to your advantage. If you don't control it, you may not end up with the brand you want. You can also control the volume of your brand. Maybe you need to turn up the volume, or exaggerate your brand a little to ensure it stands out from the rest.

Just like Apple cannot change its brand to match IBM (or vice versa), you cannot make your brand be something you're not. Your own personal values are part of your brand. If you are a conservative, honest, private, down-to-earth kind of person, you won't be successful if you attempt to base your brand around being a wild, aggressive, over-the-top, wheeler-dealer type. If it's not you—not your true self—then it won't come off well. That would be like sticking a BMW logo on a Kia and expecting people to believe the quality of Kia is equal to that of BMW. Behind its back, people would still say the Kia has the quality of a Kia, no matter what logo you put on it.

When developing your brand, ask yourself who you really are. What do you stand for? What do you believe in? What are your values? What makes you different from other drivers (other than the obvious, that you are faster than any one else!)? One of the most important aspects of understanding your brand is the need to be authentic. If not, people will see you as a phony (which, by the way, is a brand attribute—not a good one, but one nonetheless).

Are you a fun person, or a more serious one? Are you conservative or a wild one? A risk-taker, or a calculating person? An outgoing, talkative, and colorful person, or more introverted and keep-to-yourself type? What's important to you—honesty, having fun, smart decision making, a business-like attitude, trusting of your intuition, and/or thoughtfulness? These are just a few questions you should ask yourself, for they will help you create a brand that best reflects your personality. Then you can begin to tune it up or down to suit your business plan.

Remember, you can't be all things to all people. You need to be yourself and define those parts of yourself that make you different from the pack. Once you're clear on that, you need to focus on building your brand around those characteristics.

Chapter 9

"Sponsors"

We hate the terms "sponsor" and "sponsorship." To us, a sponsor is a company that provides some money (or other thing of value) in return for a "warm and fuzzy" feeling. In other words, a sponsor doesn't make the decision to be involved for solid business reasons. A sponsor is a company that pays for the local softball team's uniforms. It's done more for goodwill than for return on investment.

In racing, the companies that get involved for solid business reasons are business partners. They are using the sport as a means to improve their businesses, either through marketing or straight business-to-business objectives. Goodwill and feeling good has nothing to do with it.

Unfortunately, the terms sponsor and sponsorship are ingrained in the minds of everyone in motorsport. We say unfortunately because we believe it subconsciously gives people a mindset that is unfavorable. It takes away the sense of responsibility of providing value from the people selling and servicing the marketing program, even if they don't realize it. By calling it what it is—a marketing program, a partnership, a business-to-business investment—one immediately feels the sense of responsibility to focus on providing value. And that's when good things happen.

Perhaps we're wrong to do so, but for simplicity, we will refer to a business or marketing partner every now and then as a sponsor, simply because it's so common. It's a bit like referring to a Kleenex. While not all tissues are Kleenex, it's the commonly used phrase or term. We'll often use the common term "sponsor."

Having said that, it is your responsibility of providing something of value that will help you more than anything else in selling a program.

The sooner you focus on what the company or individual wants and forget about your needs, the sooner you will sign a partner who will join your team. And that's also how you need to look at it; your business partner is part of your team, and you're part of his team. In fact, together you are a team.

Far too many drivers attempt to sell a program by asking for what they want. The driver walks into a company and tells it that if it provides X-amount of money, he will race here and there and win this many races. Who cares? Not the company you're talking to. What does it care about? It cares about what you can do for the company, and how providing you with financial support will advance its goals or products.

SPEED SECRET #21

It's not what you want; it's what the "sponsor" wants.

So, before you begin looking for sponsorship support, you need to do a little self-appraisal of what you have to offer, and then think like a business owner. Imagine yourself in the shoes of the owner, or shareholders, of a company, and ask yourself if you would buy what you're selling.

The complete process of getting and keeping a marketing or business partner can be broken down into these steps:

1. Prepare
2. Prospect
3. Sell
4. Service

Preparation

The first step we recommend to every driver is to learn as much as you possibly can about marketing and the whole sponsorship world. A few basic marketing classes would be a great place to start. If nothing else, they can help you learn the language of marketing professionals and the basic concepts of the field.

You should begin to read as much as you possibly can about marketing and sponsorship. There are a few books that focus just on

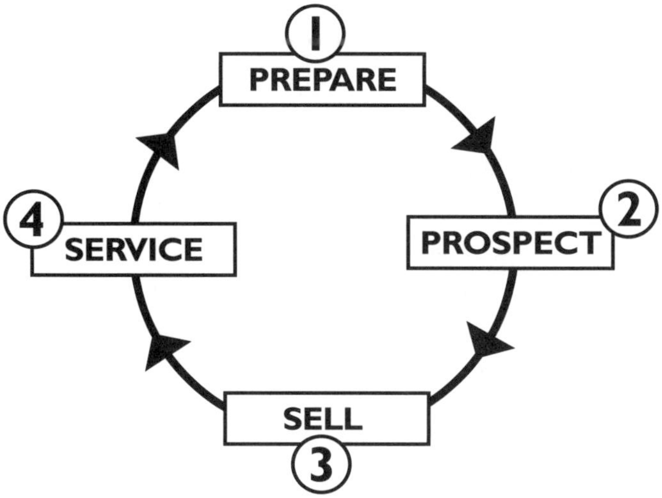

Selling a sponsor program is just one step in the process. Also note that the process never ends. Once you've acquired a sponsor, you must then service the program and be prepared to do it all over again for the following year.

motorsport marketing/sponsorship, which we've listed in the back of this book.

You should also read magazines and newspapers like *Wired, Business 2.0,* and *The Wall Street Journal* to ensure you're up-to-date on what's happening in the business world. Find out what the latest trends are, which companies are doing well and why, and who the movers and shakers are in the business world.

Learn what resources are available to you. Books with lists of advertisers are available in most libraries. Annual reports on many companies are available by request from the companies themselves. Company financial reports are available online. Search Google to find other online sources. Use these resources when researching for what you can do for a marketing partner.

Learn what you and your series can offer a company from a marketing and/or business perspective. You should develop a menu of items. Not all will fit every company, but most will work for at least one company. Brainstorm to come up with every conceivable use of your motorsport program so you're prepared to work with any company. And if, "name on the car" is on the list, go back and think again.

Understand that a company's name on the side of race car should be no more than the starting point. If your entire program is based on the exposure a company is going to get from its name on the car, then you will rarely ever sell it. Think of any exposure a company gets from its name on the car as a bonus.

Chances are you know someone in marketing. Give this friend a call and explain what you're trying to do. See if you can buy this person lunch and try to get some insights on his complicated and interesting profession. Learn what pros do to attract people to a particular product. People like to share their expertise, and as long as you're pleasant, appreciative, and don't take more than you give, you can learn something and maybe derive some mutual benefit.

SPEED SECRET #22

A logo on the side of a race car typically provides as much value to a sponsor as the cost of the sticker itself.

So, why do companies sponsor race drivers and teams? Here are just a few of the big picture reasons (you will need to further define each one to fit your program and get more specific):

- Reinforce market position
- Develop brand and brand recognition
- Reinforce brand attributes
- Buy or build audience
- Create product/service trial opportunities
- Generate sales
- Generate business-to-business opportunities
- Build relationships
- Community involvement
- Provide access to new markets
- Cross-promotion opportunities
- Company morale-boosting

The next question you need to ask yourself is if you can work with a company in trade for product or service instead of just cash—in other words, soft dollars rather than hard dollars. For example, could you build a program around hotels being supplied to the team for the season? And if so, what value does that represent in dollars? For many companies, trading product or services is less expensive than a cash investment, and therefore it may be an easier sell.

One of the first things most racers focus on is the package of information they are going to use to sell themselves. We're not saying it should be the first thing, as we think it has little to do with the selling of your program, but it's the place many racers start.

We refer to this information that you present to a company or individual as a package, as it can take on a variety of looks and forms. It can be as simple as a letter or as complex as a video/DVD presentation; it could be a folder with a number of pages or a bound booklet. How you choose to present your information will mostly be dependent on your (or your advisor's) expertise and budget.

So, no matter if your presentation is on paper, a CD/DVD, PowerPoint, or delivered by a pack of dancing dogs in tutus, it's just a package of information. And there's one very important point you must never forget: it's not the presentation of your program that's going to make the sale, it's the content of the program. If what you are offering is not what the company wants, no amount of flashy presentation is ever going to convince it to help you.

True, ultimately it is the presentation and the content that make the sale. One helps you get in the door. The other keeps it from being slammed in your face. But in the end, there are really two things that will make or break the sale of a motorsport marketing program: you, and the quality and content of the program you're offering. Many drivers would do better to spend more time on developing the content of the program, and less time on the presentation of it.

This is not to say that the presentation is unimportant. We've seen presentations with the name of the prospective company misspelled on the front cover; it looked like a fourth-grade student had written it. But ultimately, it wasn't the fact that the presentation wasn't flashy that made the companies say no to it. It was what the package said about the person behind it and what the presentation was offering that made the difference. If the person was not committed enough to proofread his package, what does that say about his commitment to providing the company with what he promises?

A simple, well-written letter presenting a program that provides real value to a company will always sell before a flashy, multimedia presentation with little to no substance. Again, it's you and the content of your program that is going to make the difference.

Again, we want to make this clear: the presentation of the package is important, but a great presentation will not sell the program on its own. The offer, the content, the presentation, and you are what matter. Therefore, before you pay a marketing company a few thousand bucks

Sponsorship is much more than just a logo on the side of a car. If that's the only justification you have for a company to sponsor you, get used to paying for your racing out of your pocket! Real marketing programs rely on a variety of strategies to make it work, from show cars to innovative product packaging and beyond.

to prepare a flashy, glossy promotional package, make sure the content meets the recipient's and your needs and vision.

In general terms, there are two types of packages you may need in your search of marketing partners. The first is designed to be presented to companies and individuals who have little to no understanding of the sport and how it can be of benefit to them. Its primary objective is to sell them on the concept of motorsport marketing—the whys and hows of it. This is for companies and individuals who need to be convinced of the benefits of an involvement. Not surprisingly, this package should have less about you and more about motorsport marketing.

The second type of package is designed for companies or individuals who already know the benefits the sport can offer. Mostly, these companies and individuals are already involved in racing, and rather than having to be sold on motorsport marketing, they simply need to be sold on you. For example, sending a package of information to Interstate Battery or Miller Brewing Company telling it of all the benefits motorsport can bring it will probably do more harm than good. Both companies already know how to use motorsport to market their products. What they need to be sold on is why and how you are going to do a better job of doing that than some other driver.

Obviously, this type of package should be more about you and what you can offer than on selling the concept of motorsport marketing.

So, what should be included? Every package is unique, but the basics are:

- How motorsport marketing works
- How the company can benefit from a motorsport program
- What your specific program has to offer
- What makes you/your team better/different from others—the hook
- A little background on the series, car, etc.

Of course, how much detail you go into on each of the above subjects is dependent on which company the package is aimed at. If it's a company that already knows how to use motorsport as a business tool, then you should put more emphasis on selling yourself and your team. If the company knows very little about motorsport and how it can be used, then that information must make up the majority of the package. In other words, you have to customize the package for each and every company you approach.

Here's a common question: should your race budget be included in the presentation package? No. First of all, this is something that is discussed ideally once you've sold the concept. Secondly, it's something that is negotiated based on what you can ultimately provide to the company. It's not a one-size-fits-all situation. We don't believe you can put one price on something, because we don't think you can offer the same program to every company. It needs to be customized based on each company's particular needs.

That's perhaps the most important thing to keep in mind. If you think you are going to produce 500 copies of the same package, send them out to 500 companies, and get a positive response, then you are a very optimistic person—perhaps too optimistic. You're best bet is to customize each and every package to suit the different companies.

We also believe that the package is not the beginning piece; it's not what you use to get in the door, or to even begin the presentation. To us, the package is something you leave behind, something that outlines what you've told them. If you're relying on the package to sell your program, then you're in trouble. For this reason, each and every package should be customized based on what you learned in the presentation meeting, and then sent a day or two later to summarize the real presentation.

Prospecting

"Who do I know?" That's the first question you need to ask yourself when beginning to look for a sponsor. By this, we're not suggesting that your only possibilities for finding a sponsor are going to come from someone you know. But we are suggesting that it's the best place to start when looking for one, and that it may be the best place to actually find one.

Start by making a list of everyone you know who may just have the slightest amount of power or influence, or the slightest chance of knowing someone else who does. Then ask your family and friends to do the same thing. If you really go through this process, you may be surprised just how long a list this is. For many drivers, the list is well over 50 people in the end.

Again, all you're doing at this stage is making a list of people who may have power, influence, or connections to other people who have power or influence. We know you're probably wondering why we haven't suggested a list of people with money. Actually, we have. Most people with power or influence have money, but not all people with money have power or influence. You need people with power or influence more than you need people with money.

SPEED SECRET #23

A person with power and influence will help your career more than one with only money.

Another approach is to start with a list of companies that match well with your brand characteristics and program, and then ask your contacts if they know anyone at those companies. If you have both a company that fits your brand and program and a personal contact, then you're halfway home.

Once you've assembled this list, it's time to think through each and every person on it to see how you can connect with him, and what he may be able to do to help. For example, one person may be able to introduce you to a decision maker at a large company since he used to work there. Or an uncle may own a chain of stores and have access to the decision-makers at some of his suppliers. A friend of your family married a wealthy real estate developer, and a good friend from school's father owns three car dealerships. All of these people could either influence someone else to help you or know someone else who could.

This is networking, and getting to the person you want at the end of the network is the goal. Actually, the network never ends, as you'll learn.

So, why all this emphasis on who you know and networking, just to find a sponsor? Because randomly shooting out letters or cold calling companies is not an effective way of prospecting sponsors. Networking is something we all practice. If someone you never heard of sent you a letter and said please hire me to work on your race team, what would you do? Probably nothing, unless you were in need and the letter was particularly impressive. But what if a friend from school called, saying his brother wanted to learn the business and would love to talk with you about maybe working on your program? Odds that you would at least meet with that person are better than 50 percent. Other people and businesses are no different. If you can get a person who knows your desired contact to introduce you to him, that will open a door and you're more likely to be successful in getting what you want.

Prospecting is all about qualifying, or selecting, potential companies and individuals to whom your chances of selling your program are greatest. It's what every great salesperson in the world does. Why waste your time talking to a company or individual who is unlikely even to listen to your story when there are others who may even have an interest in investing in your racing program? Think of it like trying to sell car parts to a flower shop. There needs to be something about motorsport or you that makes for a compelling product that a company would want to buy.

Let us make one thing very clear right now: sending out bulk mailings of letters and packages is a waste of your time, effort, and money. Take the time to qualify companies and find out which ones would benefit most from your program, and then approach them. Do your research first. What type of marketing do they currently do? Are they involved in other forms of sponsorships? If so, in what areas? Sports or the arts? What seems to be the direction of growth for them? Are they expanding into new markets, ones that match the areas you will be racing in? Who are the decision-makers in the company, especially regarding something like your motorsport marketing program? What is the company's fiscal year? (Most companies won't make a decision in your favor once they have set their budgets for the year.)

The more information you can find out about a potential sponsor, the better your chances of convincing that sponsor. Compare the time, effort, and money it takes to do this research to the time, effort, and money it takes to use the bulk-mail, shotgun approach. If you compare results, there definitely isn't any advantage to the second method. A thoughtful, strategic approach will always win over quantity when it comes to sponsor hunting.

Look closely at what types of benefits your motorsport marketing program could offer a company. Be realistic. Is a company really going to benefit from its logo stuck to the side of your car as you race in front of 800 spectators (understand that most spectator counts are wildly optimistic . . . and untrue)? If that's what you're relying on to sell your program, then you better get used to paying your own way, because that's not going to sell.

You better understand every last little detail of the benefits your program could and should offer a company. If you don't, how do you expect anyone else to? Take the time to learn every possible angle you can provide a company.

Now comes the time for some serious prospecting; it's time to figure out which companies could benefit from your program. Where to start? Business magazines and newspapers, and trade journals are a good place. Follow the stock market. Make note of which company is advertising on TV or radio or in print. Ask yourself if a company trying to spread its message with ads could benefit from your program. Look for companies that are expanding their market areas or are doing very well financially. Ask yourself how these companies could benefit from your program.

This process, the prospecting of potential sponsors, could be the single most time-consuming part of acquiring one. But it may also be the most important.

With any luck at all, if you match up the benefits your program offers with the companies on your potentials list, and then with the people you have some connection with, then you'll find maybe two that show up. They are your very best opportunities for landing a sponsor. They are the ones you'll need to research further.

Get the annual reports from these companies, and learn as much as you can about their financial status. Get a feel for what they spend on marketing, for it doesn't do much good to approach a company that spends $1 million per year in total on marketing and ask it for a $750,000 racing budget. It's just not going to work. Research what these companies currently do for marketing. Where do they advertise? Do they rely on public relations for a good portion of their marketing? Do they do much corporate entertainment as part of their sales program? If so, perhaps your racing program could be a major focus of this in the future.

And again, who of your contacts could possibly help you find a way into this company? Have you heard of the concept of six degrees of separation? It's been suggested that practically anyone in this world is separated from you by only six people. Contacts build exponentially because every new person you meet knows many people. Finding and capitalizing on those connections can get the person you need to talk to for your sponsorship to accept your call or schedule a meeting with you. Think about that when trying to make contact with a key decision-maker at the company you've identified as a good fit for your program.

Selling Your Program

Having said what we said earlier about companies not becoming marketing partners for a good feeling, we must admit that many begin with someone in the company liking the sport and wanting to be involved. From there, though, it must make business sense, no matter how much this person wants it to work, if you want the program to last any length of time.

So, in selling a motorsport marketing program, the best thing you can ever do is find someone to champion your cause. The surprising thing is that this champion does not need to be the decision-maker. In fact, this person does not even need to be very influential in the company. Sometimes, the champion is simply someone who can help you learn your way through the corporate politics, and who can identify for you the real decision-maker. This is not always as obvious as it seems. Often, the president or CEO of a company has an advisor behind the scenes who has so much influence on what the company does that you would be better off spending your time getting to know and presenting your case to him. And somewhat surprisingly, the unlikeliest of employees often know this and can guide you to who the ultimate decision-maker is.

The most important thing about selling is having an understanding of the perspective of the prospect (WIIFM—"what's in it for me?"). When you understand it from the company's perspective, it helps you determine what's of value to it, and that's when companies buy.

SPEED SECRET #24
If you show people what's in it for them, you'll end up getting what's in it for you.

Many times, developing a dialogue with the president's administrative assistant is the most valuable thing you can do, especially if the assistant has an interest in racing. People like this know more about when, how, who, and where to ask than you may think. They know the pulse of the company and communicate daily with the key decision-makers, and that can be crucial to you selling your program.

SPEED SECRET #25
Find someone to champion your cause.

Let us lead you through an imaginary tale, but one with a message, and one that is a lot truer than you may ever think.

Our driver, Speed, has done his homework and found what he believes is the right company for his motorsport program. What he can provide through his racing program will fit perfectly with the company, improving its business in a multitude of ways. He's written up his program, has a well-presented package, done his research, and he's ready to sell it. The problem? He's not sure who the best person to pitch his proposal to is. Sure, he knows who the vice president of marketing, the president, and even the chairman of the board are, but he's not sure who he should talk with first and who is the ultimate decision-maker.

One day, Speed drives to the company's head office and circles around the parking lot until he notices a very nice BMW that appears to be owned by a driving enthusiast. It's got aftermarket wheels and tires, looks as though the suspension has been tweaked a little, and it even has racing safety harnesses in it. He decides to "accidentally" bump into the owner of this car. He patiently waits until 5:00 p.m. when he sees a fellow walking toward the car. Just before the owner gets to his car, Speed drives by, lowers his window, and makes a comment on how much he likes the car. The owner, feeling proud, begins to tell him how he loves his car, likes to take it to the track every now and then, and can't wait to go to Road Atlanta later in the year for a driving school. Speed responds with a comment about having driven Road Atlanta, and the fact that he races.

From there, the conversation between two driving enthusiasts takes off. At one point Speed mentions that he's trying to find out more about the company his new friend works for so that he can present a motorsport marketing proposal to them. The champion, who he's quickly becoming, thinking that it would be very cool for his company to be a sponsor of a race team, offers to help. He then proceeds to give him all sorts of inside information, like who the decision-makers are, how the company spirit is not what it once was, and how the president "is a wimp" and rumor has it that the vice president (VP) of operations is in line to take over in the next six months.

Best of all, the champion gives Speed the VP's assistant's name and offers to do anything he can to help. When Speed calls the assistant the next day, it's almost like his call was expected. Actually, it was. The champion, who works in the mail room, dropped by the assistant's desk first thing in the morning and told him about Speed and how he was going to call. Sure, the assistant's job is to screen calls for the VP, but even he's impressed with Speed's ingenuity. So, he's sympathetic and helpful when Speed calls. He even tells Speed when the best time to talk with the VP is—first thing on Monday mornings when she's fresh—and then sets up a meeting.

Speed goes out of his way on Monday morning to get the assistant on his side. After all, he's the key to getting to the decision-maker. Speed provides the assistant with two tickets to a concert that he had actually planned on taking his own girlfriend to. . . . Oh well, priorities!

Speed has his meeting with the VP, but he doesn't approach it exactly the way you may think. Not once does he talk about what he wants or needs to go racing. What he does instead is try to provide some education on how motorsport marketing works, and then he asks a lot of questions. Speed has learned this lesson: Since you have two ears and one mouth, do more listening than talking. At one point Speed asks the VP, "If your company was ever involved in motorsport, how would that work? What would the program look like?"

The VP then begins to describe what a motorsport program would have to do and be to benefit the company. She tells Speed what her vision of a motorsport marketing program is. Speed takes lots of notes, thanks the VP for her time, and promises to have a document to her within five days that he thinks would be of interest to her.

Speed then goes home, sends thank you notes to the champion, assistant, and the VP for taking the time to help him learn more about their company. Then he works on customizing his package to reflect what he has learned today. He does everything he can to mirror exactly what the VP envisions as the ideal motorsport marketing program. He puts it together in a simple, but professional spiral-bound booklet with not a lot of words, but some nice graphics to break up the text and make it easy and quick to read.

Five days after his first meeting with the VP, Speed goes back to see her again. Of course, that is easy since the assistant, who has just gone to the concert over the weekend, has it all set up.

Speed walks in and presents a proposal for a plan, based on the VP's vision, that would help the company's business improve. Remember, it was the VP's idea of what would work for the company, not Speed's. Speed had asked enough of the right questions to learn exactly what is important to the company, from the decision-maker's perspective. How can things go wrong with that approach?

At the end of the meeting, the VP tells Speed that she will have to think about it, and that she is very impressed with the presentation and the work he did to learn about the company. How can she say no to a program that is essentially her own? That is what Speed is counting on.

Over the next two weeks, both the enthusiast and the assistant do their best to help the cause. The enthusiast, when delivering mail, "accidentally" makes sure Speed's presentation is always sitting on the top of the VP's desk by shuffling her mail around. The assistant casually mentions just how nice a guy Speed is when talking with his boss.

The problem is, even though the VP is in line for the president's job and really seems to make things happen around the company, it still has to go through the president's office. That's where Speed's approach of making the proposal the VP's idea really works. In the weekly executive meeting, the VP presents the idea. Had it simply been Speed's idea, the VP would have had no ownership in the program. But since she does own the idea, when the president and the other VPs question its value, she stands up for the proposal. She sells it because she owns it.

Later that day, Speed gets a call from the VP asking him to come in the next week to work out the details of the contract as they want to go ahead with the program. Speed immediately invites both the champion and the assistant for lunch to say thank you—and maybe even a little more inside information. You can never prepare too much, is Speed's attitude.

While this story is not true in its entirely, bits and pieces of it are. It's not meant to say this is how you should exactly make a sale; it is meant to get you thinking of how you can get to the right people and get them on your side. In the end, the driver met with success because he made the success of his program about the people in the company, not himself. He extended his team to include the enthusiast, the assistant, the VP, and ultimately, the president. And he kept working at it. He moved from one step to the next, always ensuring that it was his own responsibility to follow up and take it to the next level. He didn't leave it for someone else to do his work.

Note that Speed sent thank you letters to everyone involved. Also note that this process would have taken at least a month from start to end, and that's an optimistic time frame. Most sponsorship sales processes will take a lot longer than that. They may take up to a year or more. The bigger the program, the longer it usually takes. Did we say that selling sponsorship takes patience?

If you are not a real life marketing professional or one with a marketing degree, be careful you don't try to come off as something you're not. You are better off admitting that you are a winning race driver who has studied marketing, but who doesn't know it all, rather than trying to bluff your way through it. If you take the honest approach and ask a lot of questions, you'll be surprised at the number of people who will respect you more and want to help. It's human nature, and you can use it to your advantage.

Deciding who the right person to sell your program to is a challenge, especially if you cannot find yourself a champion to give you the inside scoop. As a general rule, if your program is more of a marketing proposal, then you will need to sell it to the marketing department. If it's a business proposal that involves business-to-business or corporate entertainment, then you need to approach a vice president, president, or CEO (depending on the size of the company).

SPEED SECRET #26

If it's a marketing opportunity, sell to the senior marketing person. If it's a business opportunity, sell to the senior business person.

At some point you are going to have to answer the question, "Are you going to win every race?" If you happen to be a driver who is at the stage where you do win a lot, this is a question you look forward to. But if you're relatively inexperienced, or you've just taken a step up and it may be difficult for you to win at this level right away, what do you say? This is a key reason why your program should work from a business standpoint for your sponsor before you ever get on the track. If the only way the sponsor is going to get value from the program is when you win, you're in big trouble. That is something that you cannot guarantee to deliver.

Ideally, you've designed your program in such a way that the answer will be, "If you look at what we're offering, whether I win or not is immaterial. This program works before I ever get on the track, and when I win, it will be a bonus. But, by the way, you're not getting involved with a loser. Look what I've done in the past. . . ." Having said that, even if you have to show how you've won in other sports, it shows that you know how to win. Companies like to be involved with winners, so find something you can win at to demonstrate this trait.

Be prepared to answer the question about winning, because it will come up.

The day you decide you're going to find a marketing partner is the day you begin to hear the word "no" more than any other word. And that's not a bad thing. You see, selling a motorsport marketing program is simply a matter of numbers. If you prepare properly and learn from your past successes and mistakes, then it's only a matter of time before you have a company or individual say "yes."

Be prepared to hear "no" a lot and learn from each one. Find out why you were told "no" to your proposal, improve your presentation and offer, and move onto the next one. If you do this long enough, and learn along the way, you will eventually get a "yes."

Every time someone says "no" to you, realize you are just that much closer to getting a "yes." A "no" means, "What can I learn?" and "I'm one step closer." Sure, that's hard to buy when you've just gotten another "no" and you're two weeks away from the first race of the season without the budget to run. But focusing on the alternative sure isn't going to help. In fact, it will hurt. If you walk into your next prospect's office still thinking about being turned down by the last one, then you're going to sound desperate and will probably act like a loser without even being aware of it. People rarely buy into someone who sounds and acts like a desperate loser.

Most successful salespeople, no matter what they're selling, will tell you it's a numbers game. There is some magic ratio of the number of "no" responses you need to hear before you get a "yes." In the sponsor-hunting category, some will say it's just a matter of getting through 100 "no" responses before you'll get your "yes." We can't tell you whether that ratio is 100:1, 200:1, or 1000:1, but we do know it's just a matter of time before you get the answer you're looking for. That is, if you learn from each and every negative response.

When you've just gotten a "no," ask what you can learn from the experience, chalk that up to being even better prepared for the next sales pitch, and realize you are that one step closer to getting the "yes."

The way the numbers really work is something along these lines. You start with a list of 1,000 companies. You filter them down to 100, based on whether they fit your brand, what you have to offer, their location, any contacts you have within the company, and other factors. You then make calls to these 100 companies and get the opportunity to meet with 10. From those 10, you end up with three that are interested in discussing your program in more detail. From those three you end up with one company that agrees to put together a program with you.

Oh, one last thing, and a very important one. Ask for the money! Too many people get so caught up in the process of selling that they forget to ask for the money. You have to close the sale to make it real.

If that sounds like too much work for you, it may be time to find another sport.

Servicing

Which do you think is more difficult, getting a marketing partner or keeping one? We bet you chose the first option. You may be right, and that's exactly why it's so important you don't forget that once you have a partner, you must service that relationship. You must take care of your partner and make sure you more than deliver on your promises.

The first step in doing this begins before you ever sign a contract with a partner. If you have any interest in your marketing partnership lasting a long length of time, you need to promise 10 things and deliver 12. If you promise 12 things and deliver 10, you will have an unhappy partner and your relationship will not last. The problem is that most people, in the passionate attempt to make the sale, will promise too much. They may even promise things that they could never deliver, but they so desperately want to make it work that they will do or say almost anything. That, you need to resist.

SPEED SECRET #27

Always deliver more than you promise.

If you can go into the program presentation and negotiation stages with the discipline to promise only what you absolutely know you can deliver, and maybe even hold back one or two things, then you have the opportunity to deliver more than expected. It puts you in a powerful position. It's certainly the best place to start when negotiating an extension on the contract. Once you know exactly what you need to deliver on, find at least two things that you did not promise and deliver them. Again, under-promising and over-delivering is the key to a long, successful partnership.

The next step in servicing your partner is during the contract stage. Make sure everything—and we mean everything—is spelled out clearly in the contract. More partnerships have been ruined by a misunderstanding than by anything else. If the contract is clear about what is expected on both sides, then servicing the partner is relatively easy—just follow the contract. If there is even one little thing that your partner is expecting, but you either didn't know about it or can't deliver it, then you're in trouble.

Even if you know that you're expected to provide something that you can't, you can at least deal with it up front. Most partners will be sympathetic to this. They won't be understanding, though, about not getting what they thought you had promised and that you simply ignored because you didn't know you had.

As we said earlier, there is never a time that you don't need a contract.

The next stage is the longest one, although the simplest if you did your homework to begin with and knew that you could deliver on your promises. It's the toughest if you can't deliver (shame on you for promising something you can't fulfill).

The second you have your signed contract in hand—and probably even before then—write out a plan for how you will deliver on your promises, and then follow it. If you wait to react to things as they come up, it's a lot like not looking far enough ahead on the track. By the time you see where you're going, you may be tangled up in a crash. Having a plan is critical. Then execute it.

You may be thinking, "How hard can it be to service a sponsor? I just go out and race to win." Very few marketing partnerships are that simple. If it's a true business deal, you will most likely be committed to a set number of appearances or speeches. You may have to write something for the company newsletter and provide a hospitality package with tickets and catering. You also may have to be at show car displays and media conferences, or facilitate business to business contacts, or do many other services.

When delivering more than you promised, you could, in a feature story in a major magazine, talk all about your partners' products or services, or you could provide them with a contact that leads to a piece of business they had never before even realized was there. How you manage all of those things, and how you deliver on more than you promised is the real key to a long-term partnership.

If there is a problem somewhere along the way with the program, be upfront with your sponsor. If there is something that, due to unforeseen circumstance, you cannot deliver on, talk to your sponsor. The worst thing you can do is hope the sponsor doesn't notice. It won't happen. If you're upfront and honest with the sponsor, you may be surprised at how easy it is to deal with the problem.

The next to last stage of servicing your partner is providing some form of documentation of all that you've done. It could be a collection of media clippings, testimonials from company sales people claiming how much you helped in their sales process, an analysis of the amount of exposure the partner received of at-track and television coverage, or a listing of all the people that attended hospitality functions put on by the team during the season. The more comprehensive this collection is, the more likely your partnership will continue. This is the proof, and when it comes time for the partner company to decide whether to continue or not, you may not be there in person to make your case. It may come down to your champions and this documentation. Of course, if you wait until the very end of the season to begin to collect this material, you may be too late. This is an ongoing, season-long project.

The final stage of servicing your partner is asking for the relationship to continue. Many people are afraid to ask this question, mostly because of their fear of being turned down. If you've made it this far and delivered on what you promised, you shouldn't be anxious about being turned down. If you have that fear, it probably means you haven't done a good job of servicing your partner. And what are you thinking, anyway? That the company will turn you down if you ask because it's unhappy, but it'll magically continue the contract if you keep your mouth shut? Racing costs real money. Your partner is not going to rubber-stamp something if you tiptoed out of your last meeting. Be upfront. Service the sponsor. Ask for the money. Ask to extend the relationship.

Sponsor Hunters

Up to this point, we've gone on the assumption you're prospecting, selling, contracting, and servicing your marketing partners yourself, and that you do not have an agent or manager doing this for you. There is another option, and that's hiring an agent, manager, or sponsor hunter. Let's look at the advantages and disadvantages of hiring someone versus doing it all on your own.

The number one advantage of having an agent/manager or sponsor hunter is that it's often easier for someone else to sell you. At least, that's the way it is for most people. Your representative provides impartiality to the presentation. The agent/manager can talk about you in a way that seems to provide more expertise, as well. As an outsider and a marketing expert, he can talk with the company's people from a position of strength, and thus leave you in your position of strength, as the race driver. It only makes sense that you can't be both the best race driver in the world and a marketing expert, right?

On the other hand, only you can truly sell your commitment, dedication, and passion. And that, oftentimes, is what makes the difference in selling the program. People invest in people. Sure, your program and what you offer has to make good business sense, but rarely has a program been sold without someone with passion driving it being involved. Since you have the most to gain or lose, you will always have more drive when it comes to making it work.

Some agents/managers will promise anything to a company to make the sale, even things they know you can't deliver. But the key is that you have to deliver on it. It doesn't matter whether you or your agent/manager makes the promise to deliver on something, in the end the company is going to look to you. If your agent/manager promises there will be 50 hospitality passes available at each race, and there aren't, then your partner is ultimately going to look to you for an answer. So, the more you control what is promised, the more control you have over delivering it.

More than one driver-agent/manager relationship has gone bad by misunderstanding between the two parties. Most times the problem stems from a misunderstanding of who is ultimately in charge. Our recommendation is that you are always ultimately in charge. Do not let an agent/manager sign a contract with a company on your behalf. Again, promises may be made that you can't deliver. And more than one relationship has ended with financial wrong-doings—many times by the agent/manager—and that can affect your reputation (usually more than it affects the agent/manager's).

Does that mean that all agents/managers are crooks? Absolutely not. But racing is an extreme sport, and it does attract the extremes, the most extreme honest and good people, and the opposite. Fortunately there are more of the former than the latter, but you know what they say about a few bad apples.

If you decide to contract an agent/manager, then it is critical to have a very clear understanding of exactly what is expected of both parties. You absolutely must have a contract between the two of you. And, as with any contract, the main reason is to clarify your roles. Write out a list of every last detail of what you're going to do, what you expect your agent/manager to do, and have him do the same. Then, incorporate that into a simple contract.

Ensure the following are covered by the contract:

- What is the compensation for the agent/manager? (Be sure to include commission on money found by the agent/manager and/or by you on your own, as well as any retainer fees and expenses, and how they must be pre-approved.)
- What types of things can the agent/manager negotiate and promise on your behalf?
- All contracts that are negotiated by the agent/manager and a marketing partner must be approved and signed by you, not the agent/manager.
- All payments from marketing partners must be made directly to you—not to the agent/manager—and then you will pay the agent/manager's fees from there.

- When servicing a marketing partner, what are the agent's/manager's duties and responsibilities? What are your duties and responsibilities?
- What are the terms under which either you or the agent/manager can cancel the contract?
- If the contract is cancelled, who owns the marketing partners?
- If a marketing partner does not renew a contract with you, does your agent/manager have the right to negotiate with him for other drivers?
- Can your agent/manager represent other drivers, and if so, under what conditions?

During his career, Ross had the opportunity to work with some of the very worst agents/managers, and some of the best. He's had some that have helped in more ways than just bringing in a sponsor or two, while others have cost him more than you can ever imagine. So that you learn from his mistakes, let's tell you a somewhat fictitious story.

A manager approaches a driver, offering to help find sponsors in return for a percentage of whatever he finds. Since the driver is facing the reality of not being able to race without money coming from somewhere, and because the manager did a great job of convincing him that he has had a lot of success with this in the past, they agree. They sign an agreement that says the manager will get 15 percent of any sponsorship he brings in, plus any pre-approved expenses incurred.

After a couple of months, the manager tells the driver that he can't keep working on the driver's behalf without some retainer "to cover some of my basic expenses at home." The driver agrees to pay the manager $1,000 a month in retainer fees in addition to the commission on what he sells.

Every week or so the manager gives the driver a report on which companies he's approached on his behalf. Little does the driver know that the manager is also representing three other drivers, all of whom are paying him a retainer, as well. Each driver is also covering his expenses to attend some of the races so that he "can network." And each driver is getting pretty much the same weekly report; the manager is talking to so and so company on his behalf. In fact, he's telling each of his four drivers the same story.

From the manager's perspective, this is not a bad deal. He's making a few grand a month, traveling to some races, networking with a lot of people, becoming one of the ones in the know. And if he lands any deal, he gets a good commission check.

From the driver's perspective, it's not such a good deal anymore. First of all, if the manager does land a deal, who will it go to? And with the manager being as comfortable with the situation as he is, where's the motivation to really land that big deal for the driver?

Believe us, this kind of thing happens far too often in the sport. If you're going to contract an agent/manager, check that person out. Find out if he really is going to work just for you or for others as well. We're not saying it can't work out with a manager representing more than one driver, but it's rare. Get references from people the manager has worked with in the past. And we mean more than one reference. We've checked out a potential manager in the past that gave us two people who raved about him, but then found two others who told us not to get within 10 feet of him (funny how the references he gave us said something different from the people we found ourselves).

Now, let us throw one other twist to our example. Let's say the manager does complete a deal for a company to become a marketing partner with the driver. During negotiations with the company—without the driver being present—the manager "simplifies" the deal by having the company pay him directly, and then he will manage paying the driver and race team. Despite him feeling uncomfortable about the way this is being handled and a contract that says it shouldn't be this way, the driver reluctantly agrees to keep the sponsor out of the situation.

The first check comes to the manager, who takes his 15 percent off the top and passes the balance on to the driver. But the second payment, a six-figure check, seems to take forever to arrive. When the driver asks about it, the manager blames the sponsor and promises to "look into it." Finally, with the race team threatening to not show up at the next race without a payment, the driver approaches his contact at the sponsor company. Guess, what? The payment was made on time, over a month ago.

Finally, after much fighting, the manager's contract is terminated, and the sponsor is convinced to send the checks directly to the driver. But in the meantime, the driver is now financially in trouble, having lived up to his obligations of being at the races he promised the sponsor and having paid the team for them.

Does this kind of thing happen? Take our word for it. At some time in the future, a young driver will ask the aforementioned driver for his opinion of this manager, and he'll be told what happened. Then, young driver will say, "Oh well, he's not going to cost me a penny unless he sells something. I'm just paying him a commission."

While the cycle may or may not continue, there are people who will do you more harm than good. While you think the person is not going to cost you anything, they will; they'll cost you your time and possibly your reputation. Be very careful. Those are two of the most important things you have.

Before we begin to sound like the proverbial bitter old driver who's been taken advantage of, let us make it clear that not all agents/managers are like this. There are many excellent ones out there. You just have to take the time and make the effort to find them, to do the research to ensure they are good, and then to learn to work with them. In fact, some of the people we most respect in the world began as agents/managers for Ross. Good ones are not just good, they're great.

Chapter 10

Selling Yourself

In the previous chapter we discussed selling sponsorship. In this chapter we're going to talk about selling yourself. Ultimately, this may be a more important role than the selling of sponsorship.

When we say selling yourself, who do we mean selling yourself to? We mean race teams, marketing partners, the media, race series, VIPs who can influence your career . . . in fact, anyone who can improve your career.

Obviously, to whom you're selling yourself will determine exactly how you do it. You're not going to sell yourself to a sponsor in the same way as you would to the media. In fact, your sales pitch to the media may be no sales pitch at all. Sometimes, trying to sell them on who you are and what you can do may actually be a negative. The best way to sell to the media is to simply be yourself. Let them get to know you as you are.

In fact, that is the best approach with everyone—be yourself. Of course, simply being yourself but not having anyone know about you will not lead to much of a career. No matter what, you will need to get out there and hustle a bit to give people—no matter who they are—a chance to get to know you.

Many drivers have a difficult time selling themselves. The most common reason is because they are somewhat modest and don't like to talk about themselves. To make it in racing, this is something you will need to get over. How? By learning to adapt your mental programming and particularly your personality traits (see *Speed Secrets 3: Inner Speed Secrets*).

Everything you do in life is due to the programming in your mind. You act a certain way because you are programmed to act that way.

Some people would have you believe that you can never change this, but they're wrong. We've witnessed too many drivers adapt their personalities and behavioral traits to buy into the you-can't-change mentality. You *can* change. You *can* become more comfortable talking about and selling yourself. Is it easy? Maybe not, but if you want to get paid to drive race cars, there are many things you will need to do that are not easy.

Are you an introvert, shy person who would prefer not to talk to a lot of people? If so, you will need to learn to turn up the volume on your personality. Everyone has a personality, no matter how shy he is, and the one thing similar about everyone else in the world is that everybody likes people who have one. They would rather talk to a person whose personality is accessible; they don't want to have to dig at you to find it. As the other *Speed Secrets* books have said, you need to use mental imagery (often referred to as visualization) to reprogram your mind. In this case, close your eyes, allow yourself to become completely relaxed, and then see yourself in a social setting (meeting a team owner, being interviewed by the media, networking with VIPs, etc.). See, feel, and hear yourself being more outgoing than usual, in other words, being you but with a little more volume. Imagine yourself feeling comfortable doing this, and the other people really enjoying talking with you.

If you use mental imagery on a regular basis (once a day) to program your mind to be able to adapt your behavioral traits to suit the situation, you may be surprised at how enjoyable the occasional social outing and public presentation can be.

Of course, if you're an extrovert and talking with people is something you naturally enjoy, then you've got a bit of a head start. However, be sure to control that outgoing personality and turn it to your advantage. If it's over the top, then it may overwhelm some people. Again, learn, through mental imagery, to adapt your personality traits to suit the situation.

So, what is it really going to take to sell yourself? If you want a career racing cars, plan on making at least three sales calls every single day of your life. And then be prepared to make a lot more on other days, but if you average three a day for the rest of your career, you've got a shot.

If you average three calls a day to prospective marketing partners, you've got a good shot at finding one that will turn into a good program. Understand, that's at least 21 calls per week, 1,092 calls per year.

At some point in your career you will need to make almost as many calls to race teams, making sure they know you're out there. In fact, this will become a major part of your life, going forward. And if you don't like having phone calls unreturned, get used to it.

Before you think that the only thing you need to do to make it in racing is surgically attach a phone to your ear and bug people into giving you a ride, stop. Remember our earlier comment about being politely persistent. If you're not polite about it, you won't get where you want to be either.

The overall objective is to make sure the team owners and VIPs know you're out there and available. They also need to see and hear your passion and commitment to making it. There's a very fine line between pestering a team owner with too many contacts and not demonstrating enough of a commitment. If you make one phone call, and take a "no thanks" as the last word, you'll never make it. If you call a team owner every single day, especially after he has said "no thanks," you will also not make it. Remember, politely persistent.

When you get to the stage in your career when you are being paid to drive for a team, the networking, calling, and selling does not stop. In fact, the second you stop hustling and letting people know about your commitment and abilities, that's the point people will begin to forget who you are and your drives will begin to dry up. This is a full time job, and maybe even more than one. You can never quit selling yourself.

If you're trying to move up to the next level series for the following season, you need to begin now to make contact with every possible team. Get to know the team owners/managers and key personnel in each team, and let them get to know you. If you can demonstrate to them your commitment and your ability to help them, you may end up with a drive with the team of your choice.

Even if you're at the level of the sport where you're going to need to pay for your ride, this networking and selling yourself to teams is a valuable aspect of your career. It's a well-known fact that the price a rental race team asks for a race or season will vary, depending on who the driver is. Practically every team will accept a lower fee for a ride from a driver it truly wants. You can become more desirable to a team by selling yourself the right way.

So, whether you're looking for a drive where you get paid, or you're looking to minimize what you will need to pay for a ride, selling your services is what it's all about. Again, the key is to be politely persistent in your consistent contacts.

Once you've identified a team that you want to drive for, find out everything you can about it. Learn as much as you can about its past results, who has driven for it, and what its motivation is as a team (and all the things we talked about in selecting a team in Chapter 7). Take some time to make a list of the reasons you are the right choice for the team—either why it should pay you to drive, or why it should give you the very best deal possible on a rent-a-ride. This may be the most important stage, so think it through. You may only get one shot at pitching your story, so you'd better be prepared.

Then make contact with the team principal. Or, if you have some connection with someone else within the team, use that angle to get your introduction to the team principal. Just as you would with selling sponsorship, you need to think about things from the team's perspective. What can you bring to the team that would convince it that you're the one for it over other drivers. "What's in it for me?" needs to be answered once again.

Chapter 11

Public Relations

Let's agree that when we refer to public relations, we are talking about any and all communications resulting in you being seen by the public. Obviously, that means media interviews, but it could also mean you presenting—speaking and writing—to sponsors, public service groups, clubs, and so on.

First, here's a little background information on the media. There are two types of media: electronic (television, radio, and Internet) and print (newspaper, magazines, programs, and written publications). Within those two types, there are another two distinctions: general media, which caters to the general public; and motorsport media (also called trade media), which—as the name suggests—caters to the motorsport community (fans, spectators, and participants).

Presenting Yourself

The very first rule of public relations is: be yourself. Much like what we said about building your brand and selling yourself, you can't be someone you are not. If you try, you're going to come across sounding phony (for the obvious reason).

SPEED SECRET #28
Be yourself.

That's not to say you can't, or shouldn't, turn up the volume on who you are at times. In fact, that may be the best advice we can give. There are many drivers who need to learn to know that it's okay to exaggerate their personalities a little. People don't get excited about supporting or cheering for boring people. Interestingly, most media—when you are interviewed by TV, radio, or print—tend to flatten your personality and make you slightly more boring than you really are. That's why it's important to turn up the volume on your personality.

Of course, you can be over the top. If you're the type of person that is known for being super-talkative, outgoing, and having a real personality, then perhaps you need to turn the volume down a bit. People also don't like people who are too full of personality!

Part of your job, and one of the key requirements of making it as a professional race driver, is motivating people to support you. That may just mean inspiring fans to cheer for you, or it can be sponsors or other types of supporters. Your personality plays the biggest role in that area. If your personality inspires people to support you, then your career has a much better chance of being successful.

If you want to make it in racing, let it show. Let people know how bad you want it, and without sounding whiney, or like you're begging for it. Just show your enthusiasm for the profession.

SPEED SECRET #29

The media and the public love personalities. Let yours show.

Do you think a sponsor would rather support a driver that the fans are cheering for and who many people like, respect, and are pulling for, or would the sponsor rather support a driver who has no supporters? That's just one reason why this is so critical.

If you don't have a personality, then make one up. We say that partially in joking, as we just said you can't be someone you're not. However, when we say make one up, we really mean just turning the volume or intensity up on it. Everyone has a personality—sometimes you need to crank it up a bit to let people see it.

Both the media and the public love personalities. They love to see your emotion and enthusiasm. If you've just won the Indy 500 and you stand there in victory lane without a smile and drinking the milk, then you're not going to inspire people to cheer for you. We can think of a driver who, because of his personality, did just that a few years ago.

We couldn't help but wish someone else had won, even though we really like the driver and have huge respect for him. We couldn't help but think back a year earlier to a driver who had tears in his eyes and a huge grin when he won. He said something along the lines of, "You can't imagine what this means." Perhaps we couldn't imagine exactly what it meant to him, but we sure had a good idea! We could definitely identify with what he was feeling, and we thought, "I hope he wins this again." That's letting your personality and emotions show.

Of course, there is a time and place for this show of emotion, enthusiasm, and personality. In the car is not that place. That's why it is critical that you know how to control your personality traits in the way in which we described in Speed Secrets 3*. This skill can be a career maker or breaker. Learn how to adapt to the situation like a chameleon. In the car, it's all about your skill and there is no place for emotions, enthusiasm, or personality. It's all business. But out of the car, in front of the public, let it go. Again, it's all business, but of a different kind. Even an outburst of anger, done right, can make you seem more human and worthy of support. Some people would have you believe that you should never show any emotion, as it shows weakness. We disagree. Done right, and with the right timing, it shows you care. Suppose you've just been punted off the track and out of the lead of a race, and a TV reporter puts a microphone in your face. If you are emotionless, then it says to us that you don't care. Even if you care deeply, without your emotion coming through, it seems you don't. It would make us not want to support you as much as if you showed just how much you cared.*

Years ago, there was a professional tennis player who had a habit of screaming and yelling at linesmen and judges. He would have temper tantrums, yell obscenities, and throw his racket in disgust if he made an error or a call went against him. Most people still remember John McEnroe for two reasons. The obvious reason was his terrible behavior. The other, though, was that whether you liked him or hated him, you had to respect his absolute passion and burning desire to win every single point.

Let's be perfectly clear here: we are not suggesting that you should behave like John McEnroe! But by allowing your passion and desire to show through, you will make more of an impression on the world.

Moving from the tennis world and back to motorsport, there is a current F1 driver who is on the opposite end of the spectrum from McEnroe. Kimi Raikkonen. While you may like him, it's difficult to get excited when you see him being interviewed.

Of course, there is a balance here. If you go off the deep end, ranting and raving and blaming everything on everyone else, then you won't gain any respect or support. You will lose it. If you never show your emotions, people will have a harder time getting behind you passionately.

Speaking of blaming others, if you should ever be interviewed just after an incident on the track, don't put the blame on anyone else, even if everyone knows whose fault it was. There are far too many times when what you felt was the cause of a crash ended up not being the real cause. If you're quick to blame someone else, you could come across looking pretty dumb. If it was obvious as to what happened, you don't need to say anything more. The viewers and announcers will have seen everything, so they won't need you to tell them what happened.

If you're asked for what you think happened, you can say, "Here's what happened from my perspective. . . . I'll have to wait to see a replay to know for sure, but it sure seemed like this happened." This gives you an out, just in case you were more at fault than it first seemed to you. With that approach, even the announcers will have some sympathy for you and be supportive in how they report on the incident. If you blame it all on someone else, they are more likely to make you look dumb by telling the viewers that you obviously didn't see what really happened. When in doubt, don't say a lot. And if you need some time to control your emotions, ask the interviewer for that time. Most times interviewers will give you a moment (although they may have their TV producers telling them to get you on-camera right now!). Just remember that once you say something, it's impossible to take it back.

If an incident on the track was your fault, then admit it. It's amazing how supportive people (the media and public) are when someone stands up and says, "I made a mistake." The respect you gain by doing this will easily outweigh any negative result from the actual incident.

SPEED SECRET #30

When in doubt, don't say anything.

The media can be one of your biggest allies, if they like you. We don't know of any legitimate media figures who would go out of their way to hurt your career. However, we do know a lot who would go out of their way to help your career if they like you. If they don't, then you won't get as much or, possibly, any attention. This goes back to personality. Media figures, for the most part, enjoy their jobs, but it's still work they have to do day in and day out. If you can meet some of these people and become someone they enjoy trading a word with and enjoy seeing, then that can only help you. Even if you don't win, maybe you're someone whose view they seek out about a race or a series. Exposure for you is exposure for your business partners, which is good for your career.

SPEED SECRET #31

Serve the media, and you'll best serve yourself.

Learn how to work with the media, and you will be surprised just how far that can take you. Learn who all the media people are, not just the important ones. Some less important ones today may become important ones later in your career. Treat all media people the same—with respect. We don't mean sucking up to them, because most will know exactly what you're doing. But treat them like you would anyone else. Be friendly with them. Do what you can to make their lives and jobs easier. If someone made your job easier, then you would be more likely to help them in the future.

Finally, make yourself accessible to the media, but don't overdo it. Part of your job is to get in front of the media and public, and the more you work with the media, the easier it will get. However, if you harass the media and always beg for some coverage, then they will get fed up and look the other way. Work with the media figures and be available when it suits them, and you will benefit. Push too hard and it can be to your detriment.

Media Interviews

Being interviewed by the media can be a nerve-wracking experience for many people, but it doesn't need to be. Remember one thing: all you're doing is having a conversation with a person (the interviewer). The only additions to this conversation are a camera recording it and the interviewer taking notes (or it may be recorded digitally). If you keep this in mind, then being interviewed will seem a lot easier.

The other way you can think about it is: if you can drive a race car at the limit, just being interviewed should be easy. Ross found early in his career that his interviews immediately after getting out of the car were always a lot better than when he had time to think about it. The reason was that when he'd just gotten out of the car, his confidence in his abilities was high; he was in his comfort zone. When he had too much time to think about it, he would reflect on things other than what he did in the car. When he realized this was the cause for the lesser quality of his interviews, he began mentally putting himself in the car just before interviews to build his confidence. He would think, "If I can drive a race car that fast, then being interviewed will be easy."

From an interview point of view, the most important thing you can do is prepare beforehand. Our suggestion is that you always have three key messages in mind at all times. This does not mean memorizing everything you'll ever say. That would make you sound impersonal. There is a big difference between memorizing and preparing, and you want the latter.

So, develop three key media messages and have them ready at all times. What do we mean by that? The three messages should involve something related to your hook, something related to your sponsors, and one other interesting point. If you have these messages on standby at all times, you will not only be ready, you will also feel ready. And that may be the most important factor of all.

Think about it. When you have three messages that you have programmed and ready, no matter what someone asks you, you will feel ready to deal with it. You won't feel nervous, because most nervousness comes from the deep-down feeling that you're not prepared. If you prepare by having three messages memorized, you will be far less nervous.

We'll use an example to demonstrate why these key messages are so important. Imagine winning your first race in a new series. While you are standing on the top of the podium, the track announcer sticks a microphone in your face and asks you how the race went. Unless you're a natural in being interviewed or you've practice and prepared, there is a good chance your first sentence is going to start with, "Umm. . . ." From there it might get better, or it might get worse. Have you ever experienced the situation of not knowing what to say when asked by a track announcer or media person to speak?

If you have experienced the fear when put on the spot with a microphone or TV camera, then you know exactly what we're talking about.

Start to develop your key messages by writing them out. Create your hook, as you would say it; figure out a creative way to mention your sponsors without just thanking them; and think of at least one interesting fact about your career or current racing results. Work them out on paper and memorize them.

Once you've gotten your key messages together, stick to them. When you're put on the spot in an interview, rely on them. Don't feel you need to go along exactly with what the interviewer is asking. Listen to the interviewer's question, and then answer it with one of your key messages. We know that doesn't sound right, but believe us—it works. In fact, you'll be doing both you and the interviewer a favor. The interviewer's job is to provide a good interview, and if you change the topic slightly toward your key messages, it's only going to be better.

Before you take what we just said the wrong way, we don't mean you should completely ignore the interviewer's question by answering with a politician's answer. That wouldn't be fair. What we are saying is that you should use your key messages to buy you some time in order to mentally prepare your answer. Of course, getting your messages across isn't going to hurt!

Now we will give you an example of some key messages. Let's say your hook is that you once trained for the Olympic downhill ski team, your sponsors are Speed Secrets (sorry!) and Black Oil, and you are currently third in the series championship. You get out of the car after qualifying, and then a TV reporter is there, asking, "You qualified fifth today. Did you have some problems with the car?" You could have tried to come up with some clever answer, but instead you rely on old faithful—your key messages. You respond with, "While training for the Olympic downhill ski team as a kid, I faced a lot of extremely tough competition. I'm doing well in the championship for a reason: I know how to win, I've got a great team behind me, and Black Oil has developed some very special lubricants for our car. Along with my Speed Secrets coach, we've developed a plan that will take advantage of my background and our team's resources. We're ready for the race tomorrow!"

Did you answer the question about having a problem with the car? Not exactly. If you did, you might have made a slightly negative comment about why the car was not better that would have been aimed at your team. You also wouldn't have been able to mention your sponsors in a positive light or bring out something of real interest—your hook—to viewers.

Instead, you gave viewers some information that they will find fascinating (the information about your background as a downhill skier) and you mentioned your sponsors in a more interesting way than most. You didn't just say, "I want to thank my sponsors. . . ." That's boring. By tying them in and making them a part of your team, it's much more than just a thanks. You're telling people what they do so well. You also mentioned how you're doing in the championship, and you showed some personality and enthusiasm. That's a great start to a great interview. There's a good chance the interviewer will follow your lead and ask you more about something you mentioned, making your job even easier. And by sticking to your key messages, you have bought yourself some time to think of other things to say.

SPEED SECRET #32

Develop your key messages and stick to them.

How much time do you spend on your driving, on attracting sponsors, on developing the car? Now you know how much time you need to spend on developing your key messages, which is at least as long as you spend on everything else in your career. If you don't, then you *won't be ready for an interview, thus risking the chance that you may not come across well. How important is that to you?*

So, what about sponsor mentions? What about saying, "My Kmart-Pepsi-Havoline-Goodyear-Ford ran perfect today"? Unless you're driving in NASCAR, stay away from blatant sponsor mentions like that. The NASCAR world is the only place where that is tolerated. In many television broadcasts, the producers will encourage the pit reporters to stay away from drivers who are overly deliberate with the sponsor mentions. Find a more creative way to talk about your sponsors (and then mention them just once). You'll actually end up with more exposure for them in the long run than if you went with the blatant mention-them-every-time approach.

Being interviewed by the media, whether it be electronic or print, low key local or high profile national, can be fun . . . if you make it that way. The key is preparation. The better prepared you are for an interview, the more comfortable you will be, the more relaxed you will be, and the more enjoyable it will be. So, let's prepare.

There is no "off the record." No matter how well you know an interviewer, how low key the discussion, or how off-the-cuff it is, never make a comment that you're not prepared to see in print. It's amazing how many relationships have been damaged by someone making an off-the-record comment.

For example, you're driving a car that everyone knows is uncompetitive because of the engine. A journalist, who is someone you've gotten to be friends with through the years, and you are having a casual conversation, not an interview. He asks you why your team hasn't switched engine builders, and you make a comment about how you wish it would. Your frustration in the situation comes through. He digs a bit more and you make another negative comment. Much to your surprise, a week later there is an article on the web that quotes you as saying how bad your engines are.

This comment does much more harm than you first think. Yes, it hurts your relationship with your current engine builder. What do you think that does to his motivation to help the situation? Perhaps even worse damage. What do you think other engine builders and other teams, suppliers, and sponsors think? Their first thought is, "Don't touch that driver. If things aren't going his way, he's going to badmouth me." All because of some off-the-record comment you made to a reporter who was doing his job.

Don't be too personal. As we said earlier, we're all in favor of having a personality with the media and public and letting it show. That doesn't mean getting personal. If you start telling all the gory details of your personal life, you've gone too far. It's time to get back to your key messages. Communicate them with personality, but keep your private life to yourself.

Practice your messages at least as often as you practice driving. You may think that the drivers who come off really well when being interviewed are naturally gifted in this area. While there may be some truth to this, many have just worked at it; they've worked at it as much as they have their driving.

Just as you practice your driving technique to develop the mental programming in your brain so you can do it without thinking, you should program your interviewing skills. Imagine yourself being interviewed and that you are smoothly getting your message across, being entertaining, and generally feeling comfortable. The more you do this, the better you will be at it. Then physically practice it. Ask someone to role play with you.

Part of your job as a professional race driver is being interviewed. The better you are—the more articulate, entertaining, enticing, knowledgeable, concise, relaxed, and fun you are—the more likely you will be interviewed again. The more you are interviewed, the more people (public, teams, and sponsors) will know you. The more people who know who you are, the greater the likelihood of you getting a good ride in the future.

Know your audience. Would you answer a question in the same way for a local newspaper doing a general interest story about you and your racing as you would when being interviewed by a hard-core racing media outlet? No way. You can get away with the use of a little racing jargon when being interviewed by the racing media. But, just imagine a quote in the local newspaper such as, "We missed the setup last week—not enough stagger, too much front wing, and we needed more rebound control in the rear." What would readers think? More importantly, if that's the way you spoke throughout the interview, it's most likely it wouldn't be used at all. The editor or producer would decide that the audience wouldn't understand and would refuse to use it.

Learn to describe your sport in a way that the most uneducated (in racing terms) person would understand. Learn to simplify what you do; turn it into layman's terms. If you don't, then you may wonder why your comments never get quoted.

Know your interviewer. If possible, learn something about the person interviewing you. If the person is typically very supportive of drivers in your position, then you will say things differently than if the interviewer is the type that generally looks for the dirt.

There are racing media people who have reputations for trying to help drivers climb the career ladder. There are some who could care less about you and your career, because they just are doing their job. (Actually, it's pretty rare that someone is in the racing world without having some interest in it, but it does happen a lot with local sports reporters assigned to cover the race you're competing in.) If you know the media person cares about racers reaching their goals, you might steer your conversation in a different direction than you would with a stick-and-ball sports reporter.

Know your message. As we said, the better prepared you are, the better your interview will be, and the easier it will be. And the most important thing you can do to prepare is know what you're going to talk about. If you wait until you're asked a question, there's a very good chance you'll stumble. And even worse, you'll be sitting there for an hour afterwards, asking yourself why you didn't say this and that about your sponsors and team.

When we say, "Know what you're going to say," we mean know your key messages. If you have that, at the minimum, you'll feel prepared and be able to morph them into the answers to practically any question you're asked. This doesn't mean don't answer the questions asked by the interviewer. This doesn't mean you should be so focused on simply what you've prepared that you don't act and answer the questions naturally. But if you know you're going to be in a media conference or be interviewed by a newspaper reporter soon, think through as many questions that you think you could be asked as possible. Prepare.

Also, whenever you're being interviewed, whether on-camera or not, sit up straight and let the interviewer know you care. Show interest. Show enthusiasm. If you're slouching or too laid back, it makes people think you'd rather be somewhere else. Perhaps you would, but don't let others know.

Keep your eyes on the interviewer. In a similar vein, look your interviewer in the eyes, and truly listen to his questions. When your eyes are darting around all over the place, or staring off in another direction, it's another sign you'd rather be somewhere else. It's also distracting and annoying to people watching. And don't look and talk directly to the camera. We're not suggesting you should stare at your interviewer, but keep eye contact.

Speaking of eyes, take your sunglasses off when being interviewed, whether on camera or not. The reason is that much of your communication is done through your eyes. Without seeing your eyes, the interviewer or the public may misinterpret your answers. Also, zip up your driver's suit.

Consider how a joke or comment along with a facial expression may not come across in a print format. Don't blame a writer for misinterpreting and printing a comment or a shrug of the shoulders. You need to know who you're talking with and act accordingly.

Control your hands. While showing enthusiasm is great—and moving your hands may be a part of that—don't get carried away. If you're being interviewed on TV, lots of hand waving can be distracting. Instead of listening to what you have to say, viewers may end up paying more attention to your hand movements. And never cross your arms. It looks defensive and unfriendly.

Listen to the entire question. More than one embarrassing moment has been caused by someone not listening to the entire question. He thinks he knows what the interviewer is going to ask, and he begins answering the wrong question. Not only is this impolite, it can also make you look less than smart. Listen to the whole question before deciding how you're going to answer it.

Speak slowly and clearly. Most people, when they are less than comfortable and a little nervous, tend to speak too quickly. They also think that a few seconds of silence is bad form. It's not. In fact, taking your time, breathing, allowing a couple of seconds to go by, and then speaking slowly and clearly can really emphasize your points. People will take notice of what you have to say. Upon hearing a replay of their interview, most people are shocked at how quickly they had been speaking.

Keep it short and simple. TV and radio look for sound bites. They don't want long, drawn-out answers. Answer the question precisely and simply. Don't get too long-winded. Answer it once, and then stop.

When asked a question by a TV or radio interviewer, work the question into your answer. Try to restate the question. For example, let's say you are asked, "What are your goals for this season?" Your answer should be something along these lines: "My goal for this season is to win Rookie of the Year." If you simply responded with, "Win Rookie of the Year," it's difficult for that sound bite to be used in a TV or radio report. Practice restating the question until it becomes habit.

If possible, don't take an interview on a cold call. Instead, call back. This may sound odd, but it's not. Let's say you get a phone call from a journalist writing an article about young rising star drivers for *Racer* magazine. We're sure the fact that you're being interviewed is exciting. However, take your time. Wouldn't you want to come across in the interview in the most positive light? Wouldn't it be nice to prepare?

Most media people will completely understand if you say something like, "I'd love to talk to you, but I'm right in the middle of something very important, and I want to give you my undivided attention. Can I call you back in 10 minutes?" It's rare that a journalist won't accommodate your request. Then, be sure to get his phone number and call him back in exactly nine minutes (under-promise, over-deliver). But in the meantime, you've just bought yourself 9 minutes to prepare, make a couple of notes on what you'd like to say, and clarify in your mind what your key messages are.

Yes, there are times when a media person will tell you that they are on a deadline, and that they don't have time for you to call them back. Okay, go with it right then. That's why you've got your key messages prepared, right? At least you tried.

If you're asked to be photographed, then take as much control as you can. Select your own photo opportunity; do what you can to stage the photo. That way, you get a chance to line up the photo so your sponsors' names are in view. You can also stage it in such a way that you look your best. Many times, newspapers will send a photographer who has never shot a race driver and his car. Even though he may be a professional photographer, he may not know how to get you and your car (and your sponsors' names) in view and look good. If you've done this before, then you may be better at it than he is.

Better yet, get your own photographer and stage a number of photos of you and your car. If you can provide the newspaper with good quality photos without it having to send a photographer, it will like that. Of course, then you can guarantee your sponsors are in full view.

Tape your interview. If you're like most people, then the first time you watch or listen to an interview of you, you won't believe it's you! You sound different, you look different . . .it's not you! Depending on the type of person you are, you will find watching or listening to yourself either very satisfying or really uncomfortable. But either way, you will learn a lot by taping the interview and reviewing it later to see where you can improve the next time.

If you are going into a studio to be interviewed, ask beforehand if you can get a copy. In most cases, it will have a copy for you before you leave. Of course, have someone tape it from the TV or radio just to make sure. You may be able to use it as part of your promotional package in the future (as long as you get written approval to use it).

Let's say a magazine does a story about you, and in the article it makes an error—your age is wrong, your sponsor's name is misspelled, the number of championships you've won is wrong, or something along those lines. Should you attempt to correct the error? As much as this may hurt to hear, most people reading the magazine don't care that much about the details. While they may find your age interesting, unless it is the focus of the story (in which case, it is unlikely it will be in error throughout the story), it's not as important to the reader as it is to you and your immediate circle.

Our rule is: if you can gain an advantage by correcting the error, then go ahead and do it. If it's only your personal feelings, or ego, that are hurt, then leave it alone. If you can get a letter to the editor printed in the next issue where you correctly state how your sponsor's name is spelled, then you've gotten the sponsor extra exposure. You've turned the error into an advantage.

Media Releases

Writing excellent media releases is an art, just as writing a novel or poem is. It's what distinguishes great PR professionals from average ones. But while stringing words together in a compelling manner is critical in a novel or poem, you don't need to be a talented writer to produce great media releases. Sure, it helps, but it's not mandatory. It is mandatory, however, to know what to say and how to say it clearly, concisely, and in as few words as possible.

In the past, there was an accepted format for a media release. While it's not so important for a release to be in this format anymore, in general, the following should be included:

- Title
- Date and location of the announcement
- An opening paragraph that states the main or key message
- Support information, usually with a quote or two from key people
- A closing paragraph that summarizes who the media release is about
- Contact information that the media can use to get further information

As a general rule, do everything you can to make sure the release fits one page; two pages are okay, but never more than that. If you can't fit it on two pages or less, then you need to further refine the message you're trying to get across. It's critical that you don't try to communicate too much information. Keep it simple, brief, and to the point.

Perhaps the most important part of a release is the first paragraph. If it isn't interesting and doesn't get the main point across, many people will not read the remainder of the release. Spend time making sure the first paragraph is clear, well-written, and has impact.

It's also important that the release has some kind of hook to it. A media release with the title and message of, "John Smith to Race at Mid-Ohio This Weekend" will quickly end up in the garbage can unless John Smith is someone very special. And remember, you may think you are special, but what about the media? Does it think you're something special?

For Immediate Release

JOHN SMITH FINISHES A SOLID SEVENTH!!!

Today young John Smith did a really average job and turned a decent result in his quest for the championship.......

Said Smith," The team did a really good job on the car and the track was fun to drive. I really like driving here. It's fun."

Ask yourself if anyone other than you will care about the contents of the media release. If the media release does not contain important information, save yourself the trouble of sending it out.

Again, you need something that separates your message from the rest. "Former Downhill Ski Champion to Hit the Slopes of Mid-Ohio This Weekend" may do it; that's different.

For Immediate Release

JOHN SMITH USES INNOVATIVE TECHNIQUE TO LAND HIS 3RD STRAIGHT WIN.

This weekend John Smith used a new form of braking to bring the #5 car to victory for the 3rd straight time.

Said Smith, "In the off season, we did quite a bit of testing with a new form of braking and it's really been paying off. It allows us to consistently out brake the field and as a result we've managed to put together a nice string of victories in our hunt for the championship."

A good media release should tell a story that people other than your family will want to hear. Find something interesting about what you're doing, like in this example.

Ask yourself, is it meaningful? Is it different? Will it catch the attention of the media? If you don't think it will stand out enough to get noticed, don't send it. And if you think it is different enough to get noticed, then make sure you go back and ask yourself again. You may think it's important, but is it really? If the only real reason for the media release is to satisfy your ego, stop. Don't send out endless numbers of media releases for the sake of pumping them out. If they are not telling the people you're sending them to something they want or need to hear, then don't do it. There is nothing worse for the recipient than to get media release after media release of meaningless information about a driver and his racing woes. Our personal experience is that the drivers who send us meaningful and timely information get the attention; ones who send release after release documenting every move they make are ignored.

Generally, media releases are distributed as a pre-event announcement, post-event result-based announcement, or announcing some special news. The timing for their distribution is important. If a pre-event announcement is either too early or too late, then it will not get noticed or used. If the post-event release is too late, then it's old news and will not get used. And if your special news release happens to be announced the same day as something bigger, then it will get lost. You need to understand and consider carefully the timing of each release.

The next questions are who to send the media release to and how. There is a reason why professional PR people guard their media lists with their life. You can have the greatest, most important story of the year, but if you don't know who is going to be interested in picking up your story and publishing it, then you lose. We recommend that you should perform your own research to assemble your media list. Begin by looking at every form of media that covers your type of racing and collect the contact information on the editors and journalists. You may also choose to send your releases to race teams, series personnel, and potential sponsors/supporters. This may help get your name out in front of potential future teams, but could also annoy people if it comes across as e-mail spam. Be sensitive to this.

Distribution today is almost exclusively by e-mail, although for follow-up media kits, regular snail mail is still an accepted route. In addition, it is important to have media kits and releases available in the track media centers where you're competing. Again, they must be timely. Having a media release about your pole position distributed to the media center or by e-mail a day after qualifying will not get you much, if any, coverage.

If all the details of how to write a media release, the timing and method of distribution of the release, and who to send it to sounds like a daunting task, good. PR is not something that just anyone can or should do. That's why there are professional PR people, and why the really good ones are worth their weight in gold.

PR specialists have a knack and knowledge for writing releases that will interest the media. They know exactly when to distribute them and who to send them to. The best ones have developed close relationships with many members of the media, almost guaranteeing coverage. That's where the true art comes in. But no matter how great your PR professionals are, they will only ever be successful if you have a story that's worth telling. There is a limit to how creative they can be.

Strategy

So, what's your PR strategy? You don't have a strategy? Well, you need one, because just sending media releases out telling of your latest successes is not a strategy.

We believe young drivers working their way up the racing ladder need two separate approaches. The first is how and when you are going to communicate with the media. By how we mean what kind of message you want to give the media. What do you want it to know about you? How are you going to support your branding and your driver type? If you are a thinking driver, or professor type, perhaps your strategy should be focused on telling the media about all the preparation you put in prior to every race. That's the story, not the results of the race. If you're a charger, then your PR focus may be on how many drivers you had passed, even though you had crashed out of the race. At least you're building your brand. If you're a personality type, then the focus may be on what you've learned from your father, or on a personal appearance you will soon be making. In any case, the key is having a strategy.

The second strategy is how you communicate with your supporters—your team. This supporters strategy is just as, or maybe more, important as your PR strategy. Once again, the key is having a plan that is going to help you achieve your objectives. If your goal with your supporters is to encourage them to open doors and help you network, then the focus of your message to them should be aimed that way. If it's an "I need money" plea (not a great approach, but sometimes . . .), then a different focus is required.

How you communicate to these two groups will not be the same. To the media, it's fairly simple: media releases, media conferences, and as much personal contact as possible at events. To your supporters, it may be a newsletter, a personal letter, a regularly scheduled phone call, a password-protected area of your website, or one-on-one or group meetings. With your supporters, you will need to determine the best way to communicate with each individual, since what works for one may not work for another.

If you decide to hire a PR professional, and we think it is a very good idea, make sure you're clear as to what that person will and will not do. If you expect your PR person to have you on the *Late Show with David Letterman* once a month, you're not being realistic. If you expect to see a feature story in *Road & Track* or be a guest on *Wind Tunnel*, your expectations may be a bit high. Then again, you may have a good enough story and reputation that these are possibilities. You and your PR professional need to lay out the plan, and discuss and agree upon what is realistic, reasonable, and appropriate.

Patience is not something that a lot of race drivers have an abundance of, and yet it's needed when it comes to building your profile using PR. We've witnessed drivers who want to get their name out there so quickly that when they do, there is not much substance behind it. Therefore, there is little impact. At times, we've had to convince drivers to wait until their story is more meaningful, which can be the most difficult thing for them to hear.

For example, imagine a young driver who has won a few races in a big-name development series. Many drivers at this stage want the racing world to know what they are accomplishing, and think there should be feature stories in *Autosport, Racer,* and *National Speed Sport News* about them. If they or their PR professionals worked at it, it might even be possible to make one of those circumstances happen. But what you need to remember is that sometimes you only have one shot at something like this. Do you want to use your trump card at this time, or wait until you've captured the championship? Are you better off to wait until you have a bigger story? Only you and a PR professional—and we'd go for the advice of the professional first—can decide if that's in the best interest of your overall strategy.

So, what's your PR strategy?

Chapter 12

Networking

People are the key to your career success, and in order to surround yourself with these all-important people, you will need to network. By networking, we mean using any and all means of communication to meet, befriend, and develop relationships with people who can have a positive influence on your career and help you achieve your career goals.When we say to use any and all means to communicate with people, we mean doing it appropriately. We don't mean spamming or stalking! We don't mean being a pain in the you-know-what.

Years ago, when Ross was trying to make the step up from the junior formula ranks to the next level, he was very focused on raising sponsorship dollars. He made the rounds from company to company and spoke with just about anyone who would listen to his pitch.

Ross was doing his homework, identifying which companies could benefit from what he had to offer. He read every business publication he could get his hands on to learn about which companies were doing well, and looked for some kind of edge or piece of information that would help him with his sales effort.

One day Ross read an article about a new company that had a product aimed at what he thought was the racing spectator market. He thought it was a perfect fit for his racing program and what he had to offer. He worked the phone, found out who was in charge of marketing, and spent weeks trying to arrange a meeting. Finally he met with Mr. Marketing. Ross thought his presentation went well, what he had to offer seemed to fit, and that he hit it off with the marketing person. He walked out feeling about as positive as one can feel when trying to sell a multi–hundred-thousand dollar racing sponsorship.

A few days later, Ross followed up his meeting, and Mr. Marketing said that he and the company president were considering the proposal and it looked promising. Ross was excited, to say the least. The following week he received a letter from Mr. Marketing saying that the company "could not participate at this time."

After feeling so positive, this came as a big blow. However, Ross followed it up with a phone call, thanking Mr. Marketing for considering his proposal, and asked him what the presentation lacked and what he could do to change the company's mind. He told Ross that it just wasn't the right timing for their company and that it was too new to benefit from his program. So Ross asked if he could continue to stay in touch with him, and re-present the proposal at a later date. He was told yes.

Every six months or so, Ross contacted Mr. Marketing, but to no avail. Finally, almost two years after his initial approach, Mr. Marketing arranged a meeting with him, Ross, and the company president. Ross made his sales pitch again and walked out of the meeting expecting the same response he had received five or six times already. The next day the phone rang and it was Mr. Marketing. He wanted Ross to come back to meet the next day to work out the details of the sponsorship. Their company was in!

After signing the agreement with the president, Mr. Marketing pulled Ross aside and said, "The main reason we're doing this program with you is because you've been so politely persistent. We respect that in you."

Never forget these words, politely persistent. If Ross had been strictly persistent, but not so polite, then he would not have signed that sponsor. If he had been polite, but given up, then he would also not have signed with the company. The right balance of persistence and politeness paid off.

SPEED SECRET #33
Be politely persistent.

Business Etiquette

There is a certain etiquette used when dealing with people in business, specifically, how to follow up with them. If you push too hard and become a pain in the you-know-where, then you'll never get anywhere. However, if you simply back off every time you hear an even slightly negative response, then you'll never make it in racing.

With e-mail making it so easy to communicate with someone, it's easy to come across like you are spamming someone without you even realizing it. If you send someone an e-mail every week, especially without asking for permission each time, then it's highly unlikely you'll make a positive impression on anyone.

Asking permission is the key. If each time you speak with someone, you ask whether he would mind if you follow up with him, then that's okay. Ask him what would be a good period of time to wait before following up your previous contact. Yes, you can suggest a timeframe. You can ask, "Would you mind if I called you next week to see what the response is to my proposal?" Or, "I understand that this is not a good fit for your company right now, but would you mind if I contacted you again later this year to see if things have changed?"

You must respect that person's answer. If he says no, that means no; don't follow up with the company (unless there has been some major change, such as a personnel change, company reorganization, change in the marketplace, etc.). But if he says "yes," be absolutely positive that you do follow up as you said you would. If you say you will follow up, and you don't, what does that say about you to the person you're communicating with?

How to Network

In no particular order, some of the people you should network with are:

- Potential sponsors
- Media
- VIPs
- Teams
- Industry/community/series

We'd like to say there is an art to networking with these people, but we're pretty sure it is more science than art. We've seen many people who are incredibly skilled at it, yet who are not what you would call naturals. They worked at developing networking skills, mostly through trial and error.

Perhaps the most important networking skill is simply looking at every moment of the day as an opportunity. If you are prepared to tell your story, you turn up the volume a little on your personality, and you are prepared by having the necessary tools, then you'll be successful.

So, what tools do you need? Business cards. That's just about it, along with a desire to hand them out and to be polite.

At the race track, networking with team owners is a delicate thing. Your timing has to be just right. If you interrupt them in the middle of a debrief or meeting with the team or sponsors, then you won't be well thought of. But you also can't wait forever, and you need to show your desire to do what it takes and self-belief. If you wait forever, quivering

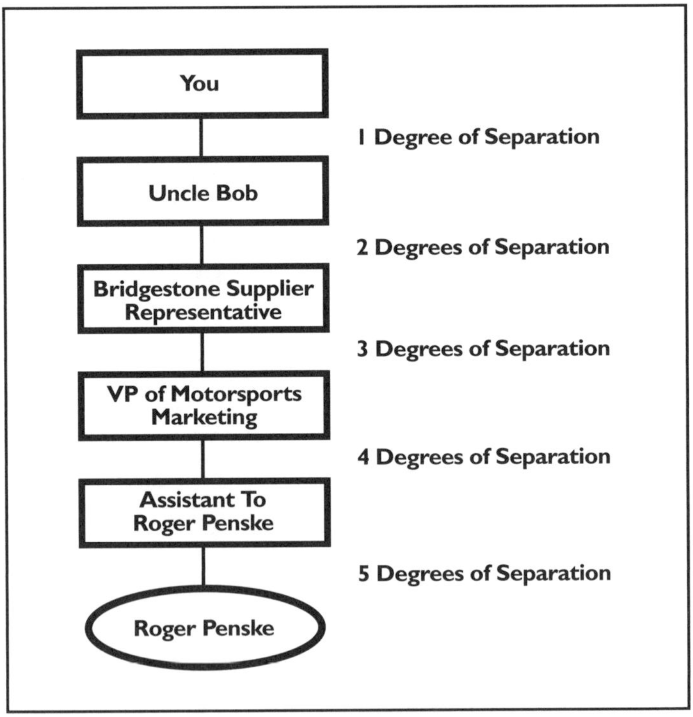

Use the six degrees of separation theory to your advantage. If you wanted to meet Roger Penske, for example, use your network of people to make it happen. It may take some time to think through how you will get to him, but it's possible.

in your boots outside of the team's transporter, what's a team owner going to think? Obviously, there is a balance, and again, being politely persistent is a good starting point.

Within your own community or the area you live in, you need to become a social butterfly. While that may not appeal to some of you reading this, it's a must. You need to find out where people—important people who could have an influence on your career—are, and then you need to find a way to get there. You need to get invited.

While there is a lot of research that points to the fact that anyone in the world is only separated from you by an average of six people, we believe that it's actually fewer than six when you're wanting to meet someone within the area you live in, and definitely within the racing community.

Before a driver attends a Speed Secrets Driver Development program of any type, we usually ask around about the driver's abilities. Even if the driver is a young karter from the other side of the country, we don't seem to have much problem finding someone who knows that driver. Within racing, we bet there are far fewer than six people between you and anyone you want to meet. It may be as few as three people.

SPEED SECRET #34

Ask people you know who they know, and who those people know . . .

Typically, the tools and methods you'll use to network are:

- Telephone
- E-mail
- In person
- At the track

While all of these methods are necessary and effective, face-to-face meetings are always the best. There is something about putting a face to the name—and the ability to demonstrate passion and emotions and why you want this so bad—that stands out in people's memories.

Contact Tracker

Name Bob Nixon **Organization** Nixon Racing

Address 123 Anywhere, Anytown, CA **eMail Address** bob@nixonracing.net

Preferred Phone Number 303-555-1234 (Cell) **Other Phone Numbers** 303-555-4321 (Shop)

Last Contact Date February 5, 2005

Purpose of Contact Introduce myself and get an update on his plans for 2005.

Results of Contact Talked about driving styles. Found out he is testing on March 30, 2005

Next Contact Date March 13, 2005

Purpose of Contact Get an update on his latest test. See if I can help out.

Results of Contact He invited me to come and watch the test.

What are you asking for from the contact? A ride for next year.

What are you giving the contact in return? Offer to help out for free at test days and a good laugh every time I call.

Use some method, either on paper or with software, to keep track of your networking. Details of the type of contact, where your contact is located, your objective, and when to follow up are critical.

Perhaps the number one tool you need to be an effective networker is simply having an objective at each and every event you go to. Sure, meeting people is an objective, but it needs to be more specific than that. Have an idea who will be at this event and what you might talk to him or her about. Prepare by thinking through what you realistically hope to come away with from the event.

Another tool you may want to invest in is contact management software. You can use this to keep track of all your contacts, personal information about them, when you last talked to them, and when you should follow up with them again. It's a tool that every serious business networker uses, and perhaps you should as well.

Chapter 13

Personal Affairs

Presentation

While many people would have you believe that your personal presentation is not all that important, we completely disagree. It is critically important.

As we've stressed in other parts of this book, the first impression you make on people will play a big role in your career. Everything from business cards to your hair and clothing style, from your marketing materials to how you talk to strangers on a plane, from how you deal with race officials to how you handle yourself in a media conference . . . everything counts. It's not just one thing that will make or break your career, it's everything.

While having a style that is yours is important from a hook or marketing point of view, understand that the racing community is a pretty conservative world. If you are too far out there with your personal appearance and presentation, then you may be left behind when the time comes to choose a driver.

Race teams will sometimes base their selection of a driver as much on how he will represent a sponsor as on his ability to drive. We're sure, by this point in this book, that you will have already gotten the point, but we've got to stress it here again.

More than one driver has had his career severely curtailed, or ended, by his personal conduct in public. Many drivers have had their careers ended by inappropriate sexual endeavors, drug or alcohol problems, or personal conduct around team members.

This has been mentioned in the other *Speed Secrets* books, but it needs to be stressed again: how you drive on the street will affect your career. It does this in at least two ways. First of all, what you practice on the street will become a part of your driving on the track. For example, if you drive with one hand on the steering wheel on the street, you will need to use some amount of your brain power—a small amount, but some amount that could be used for better things—to tell both hands to use the steering wheel.

Secondly, if you set a bad example with your street driving, there are some sponsors that may not want to be associated with you. Some sponsors may only want to support you if you have a clean street driving record. They may want to see themselves associated with a person who drives race cars, but promotes safe driving on the street.

This issue is very easy to address by asking one question: How badly do you want a career driving race cars? If you want it badly enough, then you will see how inappropriate behavior can hurt it and thus act accordingly. We, or anyone else, can't tell you how to act; but, if you want to race cars for a living, then *you* need to tell yourself how to act. If you can't control your behavior, then you probably can't control yourself on the race track and you'll never make it anyways. That may sound harsh, but it's reality.

Ultimately, your personal conduct outside of the car can have as big of an impact on your career success as what you do in the cockpit, and maybe even more. Again, it's your choice as to how you present yourself.

This is as good a place as any to discuss just how small the racing community really is, and how your reputation is critical to your long-term success in the sport. We don't care who you are or where you've raced in the past. If we wanted to, we could find out more about you, your racing experience and abilities, and your personal reputation in far less time than you could ever imagine. The racing community is extremely small and close-knit. No matter what you do, people within the racing world will know. If you "forget" to pay a bill, everyone will know. If you treat a team unfairly, everyone will know. If you say something wrong, everyone will know. If you blame someone or something for what you were responsible for, everyone will know.

SPEED SECRET #35

Controlling your reputation is just as important as controlling your car at the limit.

Licenses

We have no intentions of going into all the details of how to get your racing license, or how to keep it up to date, since the rules for this change faster than we can write. Also, what works for one sanctioning body, or one country, does not necessarily apply to another.

What we do want to emphasize here is that getting your license on time and looking after it is crucial. We know of drivers who have been turned away from a race because they did not get their licenses organized in time. Our advice is to have all the paperwork and any required medical checkup done early. Send it in early; get your license looked after early. There is nothing worse than running around the week before a race arranging a doctor's appointment for a medical and trying to get all the paperwork to the appropriate people.

This advice also applies to race entry forms and credential applications. Get them in early. Once you have your license, look after it. Make copies of it. In fact, prior to sending your license application or renewal forms in, make copies of them. This especially applies to your medical forms. Imagine what would happen if these forms got lost or delayed in the mail. If you have copies of everything, then you can at least start over with only a little hassle. You may even be able to get to a race event and use them to have a license processed right there on the spot.

Expect problems if you lose your license or credentials. If you show up at a race without them, then you will have a lot of trouble talking your way in. In fact, we doubt you will be able to do that. Again, take care of your license and credentials.

Medical

While having a medical check-up done every year or two is part of getting most racing licenses, there is more to your medical care than this. If you're relying on the once-a-year checkup to determine if you're fit and healthy enough to race competitively, then you're fooling yourself.

If you are having, or think you may be having, a medical problem, find out early if it will affect your racing. We know of drivers who don't go to their doctors to be checked out because they are worried that, when it comes time for the annual medical for their license, the doctor will turn them down. Let's see, you're about to drive a very fast race car on a circuit with other drivers running just inches away from you. . . . While you may not care enough about yourself to worry about things like this, think of what you could do to another driver if you should make an error on the track due to a medical problem or injury. Racing is serious business.

Injuries

There is a good chance that, at some point in your career, you will be injured in a crash. It's a fact of racing life. Most race drivers, at least the fast ones, seem to feel that "while it could happen to others, it won't happen to me." It's almost as if you need to have this attitude to be really fast. If you're constantly thinking you could get hurt—or worse—then you will probably be intimidated enough that you will not push the limit completely.

Racing is typically considered a macho sport; therefore if you do get hurt, you're not supposed to make a big deal out if it, right? Drivers, since they love what they do so much and because they typically are good at pushing themselves very hard, are the first to think only about how quickly they can get back in the car and race again.

When Ross' car caught fire at Indianapolis during practice for the 500 in 1993, the only thing he thought about was how soon he'd be back behind the wheel. Just over a week later, with his hands wrapped to the point where he could not even feel the steering wheel, he prepared for the final afternoon of qualifying. The thought was, if he did qualify, there was no way he could hold onto the steering wheel for 500 miles the following weekend never entered his mind. Drivers are sometimes not the smartest!

You need to keep this in mind. While you may want to get over an injury and back into the car as soon as possible, this is not always the best thing. It may be wiser to approach it like Kenny Brack did with his injuries. He took his time to make sure that when he did get the opportunity to get behind the wheel again, he was ready. If he had rushed it, perhaps he would not have performed as well, and his career would definitely have been over. Instead, he made a big impact on the racing world when he jumped in and qualified the car so well for the 2005 Indy 500.

Of course, the opposite is also true. You do need to get back on the horse and get on with racing life. If you spend too much time thinking about it, then you may no longer have the "it won't happen to me" attitude.

If you do have a crash, don't question whether it's worth being checked out. We know of a driver who was checked out after a crash, and the medical staff gave him full clearance. Later that evening, it was obvious he had a concussion, and he was far too dizzy to drive for at least a week. After about a month of pain and suffering, he was finally told he also had a broken collar bone! This driver didn't question being checked out by the medical staff members; they just didn't do a good job of diagnosing him. Imagine what could have happened if this driver had actually refused to get a medical check and had gotten back in the car the next day. Getting medical help and taking time to make sure you're healthy does not mean you're not macho. It means you're smart.

Now imagine relying on your income from driving and then being hurt bad enough that you can't race.

Insurance

Race driver insurance may be the most misunderstood and neglected piece of the driver's personal affairs. Don't worry, we're not here to sell you insurance! But someone should, for it's important.

Understand that most regular personal insurance policies will not cover you if you are injured, or worse, in a racing incident. Without some form of coverage, can you support yourself and any dependants if you're disabled? How about covering your financial commitments, such as a mortgage or other types of payments? Motorsport-specific coverage for life or disability is available. The rates are somewhat flexible, depending on the amount of coverage you wish to have. In most cases, it is also dependant upon the type of racing you're doing and your past history.

When setting up your plan, whether life or disability, make sure it covers you for any testing you will be doing and not just for race events. Also find out if it covers you when you're not racing or testing.

Perhaps the most important decision you should make when it comes to insurance coverage is from which company to buy it. The good insurance companies and agents have numerous years of experience in racing and a great reputation for going out of their way to help in the case of an unfortunate event. Take your time to do some research, talk to other drivers to find out which company they have coverage with and what their experience has been with it.

While most drivers do not think much about getting hurt, it can happen, and the real pros have planned ahead for it.

Career Options

Here's a question you may not want to consider, let alone hear right now: What are you going to do if you do not make it as a professional race driver? We know that most young drivers, when they are asked this question, immediately respond with something along the lines of "that is not an option; I will make it." While we respect that commitment and belief in your ability, you have to face reality as well.

The best approach to this whole discussion is this: You need to be positive that you can make it, but realistic enough to face the possibility that you might not. No, we're not saying you should not believe with all your heart that you can make it. There is no doubt that you *can* make it. But there is a difference between can and will. You can't control the "will make it" possibility 100 percent. You can control the "can make it" approach, though.

So what are your options should it not work out for you? Are you building a reputation within the sport that can be used in another way? We're not saying you need a backup plan, for sometimes when you have one it becomes too easy to use it. In other words, if your backup plan is too convenient, you may use it and not chase your true goal of becoming a professional race driver.

Is there a way you can take what you're learning from the business of racing and turn that into another business? Have you developed an image or reputation within motorsport that will lead to other opportunities? When not racing, are you attending school to learn a different trade or profession?

If you're making a salary from racing, or will be soon, do you have a plan to invest that in a long-term retirement plan? In other words, are you planning for the future?

Driver? Team Manager?
Publicist?
Engineer? Series Personnel?
Crew Chief?
Series Promoter?
Mechanic? Team Personnel?
Driver Coach?

There are many careers in motorsport besides being a driver. While your only focus right now may be on becoming a professional race driver, be aware of what else is out there so you have some solid plans and opportunities down the road.

In addition to the idea that becoming a professional race driver may not work out for you, think about what you'd like to do beyond a driving career. Do you want to stay in the sport? You could become a team owner or a professional coach, or you could work in the media, be a race engineer, or any number of professions outside of the cockpit. Or would you rather move outside the sport once you're done driving?

Whatever you think you may want to do after you stop driving, begin to lay the groundwork now and think how it could work for you. If it's a team owner you want to be when you retire from driving, pay particular attention to that role now. Learn as much as you can while you are still driving.

While the thought of not driving race cars may be an unpleasant one right now, as much as you love it, part of a long-term career plan every driver has to face is hanging up the helmet at some point in his life. The more you prepare for that early in your racing career, the better off you will be when you finally must retire.

Motorsport History

You may wonder why we mention motorsport history here. Having an understanding of the history of the sport is not just a nicety. It could play a big role in how successful you are in your career.

Let us relay a true story told to Ross about a young driver on the fast track to F1. At the time he was the driver to beat in F3000. He had a number of race wins in a row and was considered a favorite for a ride in F1 the following season. Prior to running the F3000 support race at the Monaco Grand Prix, he attended a party for VIPs, sponsors, team owners, and drivers. At one point during the evening, a woman approached the driver and congratulated him on his recent successes and the road his career was on, and then asked him how it felt to race at Monaco. As he shrugged off the importance of the event, she mentioned that her late husband had won the Monaco Grand Prix five times. The driver asked who he was (you can figure that out for yourself), and when she told him his name he said he had never heard of him. At that point, the woman politely excused herself.

No one knows how much his attitude had to do with it, but he never did get the invitation to drive in F1 the following season, and he quickly dropped out of the racing scene. It certainly wasn't because of this one incident. Perhaps his attitude toward the past demonstrated his lack of respect for what others had accomplished, or his disrespect for the racing community and its heritage.

We're not suggesting you need to become a walking encyclopedia of racing history. A general respect for the past and a basic understanding of some of the key events and people, and their relevance, is all you need. Read a few books. Search the Internet. You may be surprised just how much you can learn on your own about how to make it in racing. It's not going to be exactly the same for you, obviously, but you can learn a lot about the sacrifices drivers made and what made them so great. You can also learn the importance of certain races and people, which may make a difference for your career someday. If nothing else, know who won what and when, and respect what these drivers, engineers, and team owners did in the past. You never know when one of them, or someone related to them, will have the opportunity to say something good or bad about you.

Chapter 14

Last Lap

Early in this book, we discussed the challenge of writing a book on this topic. We suggested that it is easier to teach, with a book, a driver how to drive fast than how to navigate his way up the racing ladder and through the world of professional racing. Having gotten to the end, we're more convinced of that than ever!

Our main hope for this book is that it makes you think and plan ahead. We hope it makes you focus on the people on your team. We hope it gives you some ideas on how to raise the money to support your career. We hope it inspires your commitment. We hope it helps you execute your plan.

We also hope it inspires you to do what's right for you, whatever that is. The big challenge with writing a book like this is that we can't tell you exactly what to do, like we can in our one-on-one coaching sessions. All we can hope to achieve is to guide you in the right direction and ask the right questions that make you think enough to figure out your own way to the top. The good news is that many people have figured it out without any of these questions or without the guidance. After all, that's where the information in this book came from; it came from drivers who have made it. Given this guidance and these questions, you're armed with much more than most drivers who have made it as professional race drivers. We hope that's a reassuring feeling.

But having been reassured, we hope you realize that you are the one who needs to make your career happen. No one else is going to do it for you. Not your parents, your team, or anyone else. Just you. Sure, others can help, but only if you lead the way.

In ending this book, we want to tell you a short, true story. We once worked with a sports marketing person who had been extremely successful at managing the careers of athletes in a variety of sports. During a conversation, she confided that she sometimes wondered if it was worth it to be fair and honest. After all, she intimated, look at how successful the dishonest and unethical people are, and how some business deals are won by being devious and untrusting of people, and by not being completely forthright.

We then talked about how short a period of time these people survive in the sport, and compared that to the length of time the honest and ethical people were around.

After much discussion, we both realized that we had spent our professional careers treating everyone fairly, and had been successful because of it. Sure, we had been taken advantage of by some of the less-than-ethical people in the world. But we decided that even if we had lost a few business dealings to those people, we more than made up for it in the long run by being honest, treating people fairly, being ethical, and trusting our core values. We actually added them up, and when we did, we looked at each other and smiled. In the end, honesty and fair play can and will win, even in the competitive and aggressive world of sport.

In closing, we ask you to consider this, as well as what kind of reputation you want. Before you wonder if you can be honest and make it to the top, look back at the list of drivers we used in the driver type discussion. How many of those would you consider to be dishonest? We wonder, is being ethical even more important than being the complete driver? Is the reason there are no unethical drivers on the list due to the fact that they would not survive long enough to become the complete driver?

SPEED SECRET #36

Being honest and ethical will do more for your career than anything else.

Speed Secrets

#1. Use actions to turn your dreams into goals.

#2. The more complete a driver you are, the more likely you will have a successful career.

#3. If you surround yourself with the right people, your financial challenges will be taken care of.

#4. Surround yourself with the right people and your career will look after itself.

#5. Continuously look at what you're offering your team. Ask yourself, "What's in it for them?"

#6. The more variety you have in your racing career, the more likely you are to make it.

#7. The best way to get paid to drive is to be prepared not to drive for free.

#8. Look to a series where you can make the biggest impact—where you will get the most notice.

#9. Learn how to win before moving on to another series.

#10. There's a difference between competing and being competitive. Be competitive if you want a racing career.

#11. Put yourself in position to dominate a series.

#12. If you have one opportunity to strut your stuff—your speed—take it.

#13. Always be totally honest and accurate with what you felt or did not feel with a chassis change.

#14. The sooner you begin operating like a business, with proper planning and financial control, the better your chances are of a career as a professional race driver.

#15. Take your time with contracts and agreements. This is one place you don't want to be fast.

#16. Being a professional race driver is not a part-time job. Always dress and act like a pro, and you will increase your chances of being a pro.

#17. Turn every teammate situation into an advantage.

#18. Build your team relationship to the point where it will encourage you to find the best opportunity for yourself, and even help you find it.

#19. Wildly overestimate what it will take to build and run a race team, and you may actually be accurate.

#20. Marketing skills are every bit as important to your career as driving fast.

#21. It's not what you want; it's what the "sponsor" wants.

#22. A logo on the side of a race car typically provides as much value to a sponsor as the cost of the sticker itself.

#23. A person with power and influence will help your career more than one with only money.

#24. If you show people what's in it for them, you'll end up getting what's in it for you.

#25. Find someone to champion your cause.

#26. If it's a marketing opportunity, sell to the senior marketing person. If it's a business opportunity, sell to the senior business person.

#27. Always deliver more than you promise.

#28. Be yourself.

#29. The media and the public love personalities. Let yours show.

#30. When in doubt, don't say anything.

#31. Serve the media, and you'll best serve yourself.

#32. Develop your key messages and stick to them.

#33. Be politely persistent.

#34. Ask people you know who they know, and who those people know . . .

#35. Controlling your reputation is just as important as controlling your car at the limit.

#36. Being honest and ethical will do more for your career than anything else.

Resources

Books

Sponsorship and the World of Motor Racing
Guy Edwards
This may be the best book ever written on the subject, although it is very, very expensive to buy. You may be able to find a copy on eBay.

Stalking the Motosports Sponsor, and *Brand Fans: What Sponsors Really Want*
Pat Bentley (no relation, by the way)
These are great, easy-to-use books.

Get Sponsored
Charlie Hayes
Check out Hayes' website at www.GetSponsoredNow.com.

The Great Money Hunt: Without Money, You're Not Racing: An Insider's Practical Guide to Raising Motor Racing Sponsorship, Sixth Edition
Andrew J. Waite
Check out Waite's website at www.racefree.com.

Williams—the Business of Grand Prix Racing
Alan Henry
A great book about the behind-the-scenes business of F1.

The Frog and Prince: Secrets of Positive Networking To Change Your Life
Darcy Rezac (foreword), Judy Thomson, and Gayle Hallgren
Not a book aimed at racing, but the only one we've seen focused just on networking.

Flat Out, Flat Broke: Formula 1 the Hard Way!
Perry McCarthy
Perry's book is almost as entertaining as he is, and that's something! He demonstrates what kind of commitment it takes to reach the top. Read this book!

What They Don't Teach You at Harvard Business School: Notes from a Street-Smart Executive
Mark H. McCormack
McCormack created the first sports management company, IMG, and his approach to the business of sport is still applicable today.

The Brand Called You: The Ultimate Brand-Building and Business Development Handbook to Transform Anyone into an Indispensable Personal Brand
Peter Montoya and Tim Vandehey
This book is all about branding.

SPEED SECRETS

ACCELERATE YOUR POTENTIAL WITH SPEED SECRETS

In addition to our collection of Speed Secrets books, we've been helping drivers and race teams all over the world accelerate their potential and develop the skills necessary to get their racing to the next level. We offer a comprehensive collection of resources geared to assist you in becoming a more complete driver and building your competitive advantage – on and off the track. Here's how we can help:

DRIVER DEVELOPMENT CAMPS AND CLINICS

Our unique camps combine break-through coaching strategies, skills development, the most complete motorsports curriculum available plus a ton of track time.

COACHING SERVICES

Our Speed Secrets Certified coaches have worked with drivers from club racers right up to CART and they can provide you with insights and training on how to improve your skills on the track. Our coaches can work with you on a complete driver development program or just help you maximize a race weekend.

SEMINARS AND WORKSHOPS

Our seminars and workshops are a must for any driver, engineer or team owner who is serious about improving. These informative sessions cover a wide range of topics from Inner Speed Secrets techniques to racecraft, to engineering the driver as well as marketing and sponsorship.

For further information on the complete range of Speed Secrets Driver Development Services call us toll free at 1-877-773-3310 or visit us online at www.speedsecrets.com

➔ **SPECIAL OFFER for SPEED SECRETS 5 readers.**

To receive access to special offers and promotions please visit our website www.speedsecrets.com/ss5

About the Authors

Ross Bentley

Ross first dreamed of being a professional race driver while attending his first race at the age of 5, and he made the commitment at age 18 to make that dream come true. From that point on, it has been his sole focus, and he has had to learn the hard way how to make a living driving race cars. At times, Ross had to sell personal belongings to pay for the next race, work more than one job at a time, and support himself (barely, at times) while he learned the business of racing. He has since developed motorsport marketing programs that work and has been paid to drive race cars.

Ross started by borrowing money to buy his first race car, then worked his way through the ranks of being a no-pay driver, and finally became a paid professional. Along the way, he learned how to prepare, prospect, sell, and service sponsorship programs worth millions of dollars. He worked his way from the junior formula car ranks to driving Indy cars and being a paid professional driver in the prototype sports car and grand touring (GT) racing world.

As a driving coach, he has guided young drivers through career-making decisions over the past 15 years, helping them realize their dreams of being professional race drivers. He is a fanatical motorsports student and has developed a keen insight into the inner workings of the business of the sport. Ultimately, this is his key strength—a deep understanding of how the business of racing truly works.

Ross lives with his wife and daughter and runs the Speed Secrets Driver Development Services business in Redmond, Washington. He can be reached at ross@speedsecrets.com.

Bruce Cleland

While Bruce lives for marketing and business, he loves the interaction of these elements within the world of racing. In fact, he's more passionate about the business of racing than racing itself.

Bruce owned and operated a full-service marketing and communications company, consulting small and medium-sized companies in a variety of industries. Along the way, he was introduced to the business of motorsports when he was contracted to help Ross with the development of his brand and assist him with the management of his racing career. The rest, as they say, is history.

Bruce is currently president of Momentum Motorsports Marketing Services and is actively involved in the planning and marketing of Speed Secrets Driver Development Services. In addition to his work with Speed Secrets, he provides strategic planning and marketing services to organizations and individuals within the motorsports community.

Bruce lives with his wife and two children in North Vancouver, B.C. He can be reached at bruce@speedsecrets.com.

Index